D1476632

PUFF PASTRY
Perfection

Also by Camilla V. Saulsbury

Cookie Dough Delights

Brownie Mix Bliss

Cake Mix Cookies

No-Bake Cookies

PUFF PASTRY
Perfection

More Than 175 Recipes for Appetizers, Entrées, and Sweets
Made with Frozen Puff Pastry Dough

Camilla V. Saulsbury

CUMBERLAND HOUSE
NASHVILLE, TENNESSEE

PUFF PASTRY PERFECTION
PUBLISHED BY CUMBERLAND HOUSE PUBLISHING, INC.
431 Harding Industrial Drive
Nashville, TN 37211

Copyright © 2006 by Camilla V. Saulsbury

All rights reserved. No part of this book may be reproduced or transmitted in any form or by any means, electronic or mechanical, including photocopying and recording, or by any information storage and retrieval system, without permission in writing from the publisher, except for brief quotations in critical reviews or articles.

Cover design: JulesRules Design
Text design: Lisa Taylor

Library of Congress Cataloging-in-Publication Data

Saulsbury, Camilla V.
  Puff pastry perfection : more than 175 recipes for appetizers, entrées, and sweets made with frozen puff pastry dough / by Camilla V. Saulsbury.
     p. cm.
  ISBN-13: 978-1-58182-542-8 (pbk.)
  ISBN-10: 1-58182-542-0 (pbk.)
  1. Pastry. I. Title.

  TX770.F55S28 2006
  641.8—dc22

                                                                    2006025200

Printed in Canada
1 2 3 4 5 6 7 — 12 11 10 09 08 07 06

To Kevin & Nicholas

Contents

Acknowledgments

To Kevin and Nick, my two favorite guys, for helping me keep everything in perspective.

To my wonderful publisher, Ron Pitkin, for encouraging and supporting me in my cookbook ideas.

To Lisa Taylor, editor supreme—you keep me sane!

To Tracy Ford, for his great work, but also for making me laugh.

To Julia Pitkin for making all of my books, including this one, look magnificent.

To the entire staff of Cumberland House Publishing—I am one very lucky writer to be working with such talented, hard-working people.

To Becca, Sean, Robin, Kenji, Hugh, Jean, Ray, and the rest of the Saulsbury, West, and Sakanashi clans—I am so fortunate to have such a loving, supporting family.

And endless love and thanks to my parents, Dan and Charlotte.

PUFF PASTRY
Perfection

Introduction:
Puff the Magic Pastry

Puff pastry is the royalty of pastries—crisp, flaky, and especially light, it literally rises to any occasion.

And although preparing homemade puff pastry is a labor-intensive process, a 17.3-ounce package of frozen puff pastry sheets makes the magnificence of puff pastry accessible to home cooks everywhere.

All of the guesswork has been eliminated from frozen, purchased puff pastry. At a cost of less than four dollars, one package from the freezer section of the local grocery store delivers two perfect puff pastry sheets, pre-rolled and ready to use in recipes ranging from the first course to the last.

But working with frozen puff pastry extends far beyond convenience. It has an enchanting, almost irresistible allure that makes baking pure pleasure. Each frozen sheet of easy-to-use puff pastry may look like humble dough, but slide it into the oven and puff!—flaky, delicate, golden layers magically appear.

And oh, the captivating creations that await. Frozen puff pastry can be used to quickly and easily render classics such as napoleons, cream puffs, strudel, turnovers, palmiers, mille-feuille, and French tarts. But it doesn't end there: its potential is limited only by your imagination. So twist it into appetizer sticks, cut it into tartlet shapes, use it as a quick pie or quiche crust, fold it over savory appetizer fillings, mold it over casserole fillings to create one-step pot pie "lids," or roll and slice into elegant, but oh-so-easy, cookies.

As I began to develop, taste, and perfect the recipes for this book, my goal was to create more than just another collection of baked goods. Rather, I aimed to create extraordinary flavors that would surprise and delight, as well as provide foolproof instructions to make you a baking hero.

The results? How about Portobello Napoleons, Wasabi Shrimp Puffs, Dried

Cherry and Almond Baked Brie, or Spicy Cumin Cheese Straws for starters? For supper, consider Chille Relleno Quiche; Puff Pastry Po'boys; Pizza Bianco with Prosciutto, Arugula & Parmesan; or Chipotle & Cheese Beef Pot Pie. Next, the sweets. An entire chapter is devoted to sweet miniatures, such as Ginger-Lime Sugar Twists, Southern Pecan Crisps, Fresh Mango Napoleons, and Puff Pastry Cinnamon Rolls, all perfect for teatime or an anytime nibble. And finally, the grand desserts: from Lemon-Blackberry Cobbler to Chocolate-Walnut Strudel to Caramel Apple Dumplings, there's a sweet treat for every taste and occasion.

So preheat the oven and get ready to explore a wealth of baking options as satisfying to make as to eat. As you experiment, remember that working with frozen puff pastry remains simple. The choices are what will make your puff pastry experience uniquely gratifying. The recipes you select, the ingredients and baking tools you use, the people you plan to share the creations with—and certainly your state of mind—are what will make all of the difference. So unwind and savor the opportunity to bake a bit of perfection. The possibilities have never been greater.

Puff Pastry History

Food historians generally agree that puff pastry is a Renaissance invention. The French give direct credit for the creation of puff pastry—known in French as *Pâte Feuilletée* (leafed pastry) because of its many leaves or layers—to a humble, albeit genius, pastry chef's apprentice. The young man in question was named Claudius Gele, and according to the lore, he decided at the end of his apprenticeship back in 1645 that he wanted to bake a delicious loaf of bread for his sick father.

Unfortunately, Monsieur Gele senior was prescribed a diet limited to water, flour, and butter; hence Claudius was forced to use his ingenuity as much as his newly acquired skills. He set to work preparing a butter-packed dough, kneading and folding the mixture on a table ten times, then packing the dough into a loaf.

Claudius's mentor, who had observed the young man at work, warned against baking the loaf, thinking that the butter would simply melt and run out, leaving a flat, hard mass of baked flour. But Claudius paid no heed. He placed the loaf in the oven, and much to the surprise and delight of both Claudius and his mentor, the loaf baked into a highly puffed, very light layered pastry.

Having finished his apprenticeship, Claudius moved to Paris to begin work at the Rosabau Patisserie. He continued work on his invention, which earned the pastry shop both fame and fortune. He later moved to Florence, where he worked in the Brothers Mosca's pastry shop. The brothers Mosca later claimed to have invented puff pastry themselves, and perhaps out of humility, Claudius kept his secret to himself. But we can all count our blessings that he shared his original puff of genius.

What Is Puff Pastry?

The ingredients for making puff pastry remain relatively unaltered since Claudius Gele made his inaugural loaf: flour, fat (butter, margarine, or vegetable shortening), salt, and water with no leavener. What makes the pastry puff is a function of the method for combining the ingredients as well as their subsequent reaction to heat.

Puff pastry begins much like pie crust with cold fat mixed into flour to develop a cornmeal-like consistency. The major labor begins in the next stage. A "butter block" is enclosed in dough, which is then folded and rolled out multiple times, creating hundreds of very thin, alternating layers of pastry and fat, also referred to as a "laminated dough."

The real magic happens when puff pastry is baked. The fat layers, rolled in between the layers of dough, are excellent heat conductors and quickly turn any moisture in the dough to steam. The pressure from the steam, contained within each sheet of dough because it is sealed in between the thin layers of fat, also functions to help elevate the layers of pastry and set the flour's starches, so the infrastructure of pastry layers are held in place through baking. In the end, puff pastry rises to about eight times its original height. In other words, a quarter-inch thickness of puff pastry dough will puff to a height of two inches.

Ready-Made to the Rescue

Despite the enchantment of puff pastry, making the delightful dough from scratch is firmly grounded in laborious reality. Consider this description of the process from the original *Joy of Cooking*: "[Puff pastry is] the most delicate and challenging of pastries which must be made the way porcupines make love—very, very carefully."

The tome further advises to "shut off the phone for an hour or two" and explains that "in making this light and tender pastry from scratch you should choose a bright, windy, and chilly day for layering the chilled butter and pastry dough that must be rolled out and folded repeatedly."

Phew!

No need to despair. Ready-made puff pastry from the freezer section of the supermarket means everyone can make spectacular desserts, entrées, and appetizers, regardless of the weather, your busy schedule, and previous baking experience. Better still, your creations will look and taste like you slaved for hours.

All of the recipes in this collection were developed and tested using Pepperidge Farm® Puff Pastry Sheets, which is the most widely available and affordable brand. Purists lament the fact that Pepperidge Farm® Puff Pastry contains partially hydrogenated vegetable shortening instead of butter. While true, the taste and texture of the product are quite excellent, and the savings of time and energy are invaluable.

Moreover, butter-free pastry allows those who are kosher, vegan, and lactose-intolerant to enjoy a range of sweet and savory treats that might otherwise be off-limits due to dairy ingredients.

A second source of ready-made puff pastry is also well worth mentioning. It is an all-butter brand made by Dufour Pastry Kitchens. This is a superb puff pastry option. Unfortunately, it is very hard to find, both locally and on the Internet, and costs about three times as much as Pepperidge Farm® Puff Pastry Sheets. Most likely sources include gourmet groceries and upscale kitchen stores. Alternatively, contact Dufour Pastry Kitchens directly (1-800-439-1282; www.dufourpastrykitchens.com) to locate a retailer near you. Finally, if you use the Dufour brand, use your judgment with the recipe preparation and baking instructions since testing was not done using this brand.

Tips for Puff Pastry Success

Thawing the Pastry

* Ignore the 20-minute thawing recommendation on the puff pastry package—it simply isn't enough time. Thirty minutes is much closer to the mark, but depending on the temperature of your kitchen it could take up to 45 minutes. The thawed pastry should still be cold but pliable, much like modeling clay.

* Thaw the puff pastry sheets before unfolding to avoid tearing.

* If any moisture beads up on the surface of the puff pastry sheets while thawing, blot with a paper towel before proceeding.

Keep It Cold

* Avoid working with puff pastry on particularly hot, humid days.

* Keeping the puff pastry cold is crucial. You don't want the fat layers in the pastry to melt prematurely. Thaw the puff pastry until it is no longer frozen, just cold, typically 30 minutes as indicated in the recipes throughout this book. Your tools and working area should also be kept cold.

* For best results, keep *everything* cold. Use cold hands, a cold marble top, pastry board, and cold tools. To keep your hands cold, fill a zipper-top plastic bag with ice and place in a bowl on your work surface. Hold the bag in your palms for a few seconds before working with the pastry. Continue to chill your hands periodically as you work.

Handling Puff Pastry

* Work quickly with one piece at a time and keep the rest covered with plastic wrap in the refrigerator.

* Handle the pastry as little as possible and always use your fingertips, the coolest

part of the hands. The dough should be placed in the refrigerator between rolling so that the pastry remains cool and firm but flexible.

Cutting Puff Pastry

✳ Use a very sharp hot knife or pastry/pizza wheel to cut puff pastry, and be sure to cut straight down and not at an angle. Using a dull implement will fuse the layers together and thwart rising.

✳ After cutting puff pastry, the side that was up when cut should be placed down on the baking pan.

Rolling Puff Pastry

✳ Thawed puff pastry sheets should be rolled out on lightly floured surfaces. To create such a surface, dust with flour, then brush off any excess with a soft, dry pastry brush before rolling or cutting. In addition, gently brush off any excess flour from the pastry before any filling and shaping steps.

✳ Cracks may appear along the seams of the pastry where it was folded. Prior to rolling, gently press the pastry together at the seams to prevent separation of the dough and mend any weak spots.

✳ Save any scraps for other uses such as cookies, appetizer crisps, or decorations, but do not re-roll them together. Any re-rolled dough will not rise properly.

Fillings and Finishes

✳ All fillings should be at room temperature or cold to avoid premature melting of the puff pastry layers before the baking begins.

✳ Puff pastry may be baked first and then filled or filled and then baked.

✳ If the recipe involves using an egg wash glaze, be certain the glaze does not drip down on any of the cut sides. The egg wash can fuse the edges together, interfering with the rise.

Baking Puff Pastry

✳ Puff pastry relies upon even heat for optimal lift. Preheat your oven to the desired temperature at least 15 to 20 minutes before baking begins.

✳ Bake the pastry until it is light, crispy, and flaky—underbaked pastry will look doughy and wet in spots, particularly the center. Use the baking times in the recipes as guidelines, but then use your own judgment.

✳ For some of the recipes in this collection, you'll want the flakiness of the puff pastry without much puff. To achieve this, prick the unbaked pastry all over with a sharp-tined fork to allow steam to escape.

Equipment

Essential Utensils Checklist

- ✓ Dry measuring cups in graduated sizes ¼, ⅓, ½, and 1-cup
- ✓ 1-cup and 2-cup liquid measuring cups (preferably clear glass or plastic)
- ✓ Measuring spoons in graduated sizes ⅛, ¼, ½, and 1 teaspoon as well as 1 tablespoon
- ✓ Light-colored, dull-finished, heavy-gauge baking sheets (at least two)
- ✓ Wooden spoon(s)
- ✓ Mixing bowls (at least one each of small, medium, and large sizes)
- ✓ Rubber or silicone spatula (for scraping the sides of a mixing bowl)
- ✓ Metal spatula or pancake turner
- ✓ Wire cooling racks
- ✓ Oven mitts or holders
- ✓ Kitchen timer
- ✓ Cutting board
- ✓ Pastry brush (a cleaned 1-inch paintbrush from the hardware store works fine)
- ✓ Wire whisk
- ✓ Chef's knife
- ✓ Electric mixer (handheld or stand mixer)

Wish-List Utensils Checklist

- ✓ Small off-set metal spatula (ideal for spreading fillings and icings)
- ✓ Metal pastry scraper (handy for trimming and cutting baked pastry)
- ✓ Food processor
- ✓ A variety of metal biscuit cutters (for cutting rounds of pastry for tarts, appetizers, and cookies)
- ✓ Pizza cutter (for cutting pastry evenly)
- ✓ Zester

Appetizers

Blue Cheese & Fig Puffs

Simply prepared with a short list of ingredients, these are little bites of elegance. If serving for a party, you can make the puff pastry rounds several hours, or up to a day, ahead and then finish the final assembly just as your guests arrive. If you cannot find fig jam, plum jam makes an equally delicious substitute.

I	large egg yolk
I	teaspoon water
¼	pound chilled blue cheese
½	of a 17.3-ounce package frozen puff pastry (I sheet), thawed for 30 minutes
½	cup fig jam

✳ Preheat oven to 425°F. Line a baking sheet with parchment paper. In a small cup mix the egg yolk and water with a fork to make an egg wash; set aside.

✳ Break or cut blue cheese into 24 small pieces (about ¼ inch). Let stand at room temperature to soften.

✳ Unfold the pastry sheet on a lightly floured surface. With a lightly floured rolling pin, roll out puff pastry to a 10-inch square.

✳ Using a I½-inch round cutter, cut out 24 pastry rounds from pastry sheet. Arrange rounds I inch apart on baking sheet. Brush tops of rounds with some egg wash.

✳ Bake rounds in middle of oven until puffed and golden brown, about I2 minutes (rounds will puff unevenly).

✳ Transfer rounds with a spatula to a rack and cool slightly. Trim bottoms of rounds if necessary to create level pastries and cool completely on rack.

✳ Top each pastry round with I piece blue cheese and ½ teaspoon jam and serve at room temperature. Makes 24 hors d'oeuvres.

Camembert-Pecan Petites

Here the smooth, mellow flavor of Camembert, the rich cow's cheese believed to have been given its name by Napoleon, finds a perfect match with the subtle sweetness of pecans.

1	large egg yolk
1	teaspoon water
2	teaspoons unsalted butter, melted
⅛	teaspoon salt
⅔	cup finely chopped pecans, divided use
½	of a 17.3-ounce package frozen puff pastry (1 sheet), thawed for 30 minutes
1	6-ounce round Camembert, rind trimmed off and discarded

✳ Preheat oven to 425°F. Line a baking sheet with parchment paper. In a small cup mix the egg yolk and water with a fork to make an egg wash; set aside.

✳ In a small bowl mix the butter, salt, and ⅓ cup of the pecans.

✳ Roll out pastry on a lightly floured surface with a lightly floured rolling pin to a 14x12-inch rectangle. Using a 1½-inch round cutter, cut out 40 pastry rounds from pastry sheet. Arrange rounds 1 inch apart on baking sheet. Brush tops of rounds with some egg wash, then sprinkle each with about ¼ teaspoon pecan mixture.

✳ Bake rounds in middle of oven until puffed and golden brown, about 12 minutes (rounds will puff unevenly). (Leave oven on.)

✳ Transfer rounds with a spatula to a rack. While pastries are still warm, gently pull each one apart to make a top and a bottom. Lightly press down any puffed inner layers on tops and bottoms if necessary.

✳ Meanwhile, mash together cheese and remaining ⅓ cup pecans with a fork.

✳ Sandwich a ½-teaspoon mound of cheese filling inside each pastry (between top and bottom), then bake in middle of oven on the same parchment-lined baking sheet until cheese begins to melt, 2–3 minutes. Season tops of pastries with pepper and serve immediately. Makes 40 hors d'oeuvres.

✔ **Cook's Notes:** ✳ *Puff pastry can be baked and rounds separated into tops and bottoms 1 day ahead, then cooled completely and kept at room temperature in an airtight container.* ✳ *Pastries can be filled (but not baked) 1 hour ahead and kept, loosely covered, at room temperature.*

✳ *Appetizers*

Goat Cheese & Thyme Puffs

In this easy preparation, puff pastry and thyme dress up goat cheese, making a special appetizer for company while preserving the pure goodness of the cheese.

½   of a 17.3-ounce package frozen puff pastry (1 sheet), thawed for 30 minutes
     All-purpose flour for dusting
½   cup crumbled goat cheese (about 3½ ounces)
1   tablespoon heavy cream (or ½ tablespoon whole milk)
⅛   teaspoon black pepper
2   large eggs, lightly beaten
1½ tablespoons fresh thyme leaves

✳ Preheat oven to 425°F.

✳ Roll out pastry into a 14x10-inch rectangle (about ⅛-inch thick) on a lightly floured surface. Trim edges, preferably with a pizza wheel, and cut pastry lengthwise into six (6) 1½-inch-wide strips. Transfer strips to an ungreased baking sheet. Chill, covered with plastic wrap, until cold, about 10 minutes.

✳ Blend goat cheese, cream, pepper, and 1 tablespoon of the beaten egg in a food processor until smooth, then form into 21 tiny balls on a work surface.

✳ Keeping remaining pastry covered, brush top of 1 strip with some of remaining beaten egg. Starting ½ inch from one end and leaving ½ inch at opposite end, evenly space 7 cheese balls down center of strip. Cover with another pastry strip, pressing ends together, then press between balls of filling gently but firmly. Press pastry around each ball to seal top and bottom together and wipe away any filling that leaks out.

✳ Brush top of strip (but not sides) with some of egg and sprinkle with ½ tablespoon thyme. Cut between mounds of filling to form squares and arrange pastries 1 inch apart on a parchment-lined baking sheet. Make more pastries with remaining strips, filling, and thyme.

✳ Bake in middle of oven until puffed and golden, about 12 minutes. Serve warm. Makes 21 hors d'oeuvres.

✔ **Cook's Note:** ✳ *Unbaked pastries can be frozen, wrapped well in plastic wrap, for up to 2 weeks. Thaw in refrigerator.*

Appetizers ✳

Asparagus-Gruyère Spring Rolls

Flavored with fresh chives, Dijon mustard, and the rich, sweet, nutty taste of Gruyère, these artistic spring rolls are as delicious as they are beautiful.

2	large egg yolks
1	tablespoon water
1	tablespoon Dijon mustard
1	17.3-ounce package frozen puff pastry (2 sheets), thawed for 30 minutes
1¾	cups packed finely grated Gruyère cheese
24	(¾-inch-thick) asparagus (about 2 pounds) stalks, trimmed to 6-inch lengths and tips reserved, if desired
⅓	cup chopped fresh chives

＊ In a small cup mix the egg yolks, water and mustard with a fork to make egg wash; set aside.

＊ Unfold pastry sheets on a lightly floured surface. Cut each sheet in half (cut in half parallel to fold lines). Roll out 1 half (keep remaining 3 halves chilled, covered with plastic wrap) to a 20x7-inch rectangle with a floured rolling pin on a well-floured surface. (Pastry will shrink slightly after rolling.) Brush off excess flour from work surface and both sides of pastry, then trim all edges with a sharp knife to even them. Cut crosswise into six (6) 6½x3-inch rectangles.

＊ Brush rectangles with some egg wash and sprinkle each evenly with 1 tablespoon Gruyère, leaving a ½-inch border on long sides. Lay an asparagus stalk along 1 long side and sprinkle with a teaspoon of chives. Roll up asparagus in pastry, pressing seam to seal. Make more rolls with remaining pastry, cheese, asparagus and chives.

＊ Arrange rolls, seam sides down, about 1 inch apart on nonstick baking sheets. Lightly brush top and sides with egg wash. Chill rolls until pastry is firm, at least 15 minutes.

＊ Preheat oven to 400°F.

＊ Bake rolls in batches in middle of oven until puffed and golden, about 16 minutes.

＊ Transfer with a metal spatula to a cutting board and trim about ½ inch from ends. Halve each roll crosswise, then, starting about ½ inch from either end, cut each sec-

Appetizers

ASPARAGUS-GRUYÈRE SPRING ROLLS

tion diagonally in half. Stand asparagus rolls on end, 2 by 2 on platter. Serve warm. Makes about 96 hors d'oeuvres.

✔ **Cook's Notes:** ✻ *The unbaked spring rolls can be chilled, loosely covered with plastic wrap, up to 1 day.* ✻ *Alternatively, the spring rolls can be baked (but not cut) 4 hours ahead and kept, uncovered, at room temperature. Reheat in a 350°F oven 8–10 minutes.*

Thai Herb Pinwheels

The flavors of Thailand—fresh herbs and a ready-made peanut sauce—are perfectly at home in these elegant spiral appetizers.

½   of a 17.3-ounce package frozen puff pastry (1 sheet), thawed for 30 minutes

½   cup jarred Thai peanut sauce

¼   cup chopped fresh cilantro leaves

¼   cup chopped fresh mint leaves

¾   cup (packed) finely grated mozzarella cheese

1   large egg, beaten to blend

＊ Place pastry sheet on work surface. Cut in half, forming two 9½ x 4¾-inch rectangles.

＊ Spread ¼ cup of the peanut sauce over one of the puff pastry rectangles, leaving ½-inch border along 1 side. Sprinkle with half of the cilantro and half of the mint, then top with half of cheese. Brush plain border with egg. Starting at long side of the opposite border, roll up pastry jelly roll–style, pressing gently to seal long edges. Wrap in plastic. Repeat with remaining pastry, peanut sauce, cilantro, mint, cheese, and egg to form second log. Refrigerate until firm, at least 3 hours and up to 2 days.

＊ Position rack in center of oven and preheat to 400°F. Line 2 large baking sheets with parchment paper. Cut logs crosswise into ½-inch-thick rounds. Arrange rounds on prepared sheets, spacing 1 inch apart.

＊ Bake 1 sheet at a time until pastries are golden brown, about 16 minutes. Using metal spatula, transfer pastries to racks and cool slightly. Serve warm. Makes about 30 appetizers.

Appetizers

Spicy Black Bean Empanadas

Pumpkin is the secret ingredient in these spicy, robust, vegetarian empanadas. Add a tossed green salad, and you can easily transform this finger food into a quick and delicious dinner.

2	tablespoons vegetable oil
¾	cup chopped onion
I	15-ounce can black beans, rinsed and drained
½	cup canned solid pack pumpkin
¼	cup chopped fresh cilantro
I	teaspoon ground cumin
¼	teaspoon cayenne pepper, or to taste
	Salt, to taste
I	17.3-ounce package frozen puff pastry (2 sheets), thawed
I	cup grated Monterey Jack cheese
I	large egg, beaten to blend (for glaze)

✳ Heat oil in a medium-size, heavy skillet over high heat. Add onion and sauté 3 minutes. Add beans, pumpkin, cilantro, cumin, and cayenne; cook until mixture is warmed through, about 3 minutes. Remove from heat. Using back of fork, mash bean filling to coarse paste; season with salt. Cool.

✳ Preheat oven to 425°F. Roll out each puff pastry sheet on lightly floured surface to a 14-inch square. Cut each into 9 squares. Place I heaping tablespoon bean filling in center of each square. Sprinkle each mound of filling with cheese. Brush edges of squares with egg glaze. Fold I corner over filling to opposite corner, forming triangle. Using fork, seal crust edges.

✳ Arrange pasties on rimmed baking sheet; brush with egg glaze. Bake empanadas until golden brown, about 15 minutes. Serve warm. Makes 18 empanadas.

Mini Shrimp Cornets

Petite and pretty, these delicate shrimp pastries make a delightful prelude to a special supper.

1	tablespoon unsalted butter
¼	cup finely chopped onion
1	pound large shrimp (21–25 per lb. in shell), peeled, deveined, and coarsely chopped
2	tablespoons medium-dry sherry
1	tablespoon chopped fresh tarragon or 1¼ teaspoons dried tarragon
½	teaspoon salt
¼	teaspoon black pepper
1	17.3-ounce package frozen puff pastry (2 sheets), thawed for 30 minutes
1	large egg
1	tablespoon milk

✳ Position oven racks in upper and lower thirds of oven and preheat oven to 400°F. Line 2 large baking sheets with parchment paper.

✳ Heat butter in an 8-inch skillet over moderately low heat. Add onion and cook, stirring occasionally, until softened but not browned, about 2 minutes. Transfer to a bowl to cool. When onion is cool, add shrimp, sherry, tarragon, salt, and pepper and stir until combined well.

✳ Roll out 1 sheet of pastry on a lightly floured surface to a 12-inch square. Cut into thirds in one direction, then into fourths in the other direction to make twelve (12) 3x4-inch rectangles. Cut each rectangle in half diagonally to form 2 triangles.

✳ Place 1 triangle on a work surface with longest edge nearest you, then put 1 teaspoon shrimp filling in center of triangle. Bring bottom corner of shortest side up to top point, then wrap remaining corner around resulting cone. Pinch to seal, then transfer to a lined baking sheet. Form more cornets in same manner, then repeat with remaining sheet of pastry. Chill first sheet of cornets, loosely covered, while making second.

✳ Whisk together egg and milk in a small cup and lightly brush over top of pastries.

✳ Bake in upper and lower thirds of oven, switching position of sheets halfway through baking, until golden, about 18–20 minutes total.

Appetizers

MINI SHRIMP CORNETS

✳ Cool cornets on sheets on racks 5 minutes, then gently loosen from parchment with a spatula. Serve warm. Makes 48 hors d'oeuvres.

✔ **Cook's Note:** *Cornets can be formed, but not brushed with egg wash, 3 days ahead. Freeze on sheets in 1 layer, then remove from sheets and keep in a sealed plastic bag. Do not thaw before brushing with egg wash and baking as directed.*

Smoky Cheddar Palmiers

In many ways these are the perfect appetizer—or snack, for that matter. They are delightfully crisp and cheese-y, and the smoked pimenton adds a lively kick of smoke and fire. You can use chipotle chile powder, which also has a smoky flavor, in place of the pimenton, or use this recipe as a template for your own favorite cheeses and spices.

1½	tablespoons chili powder
1½	tablespoons firmly packed light brown sugar
¾	teaspoon hot pimenton (Spanish smoked paprika)
¾	teaspoon salt
4	tablespoons chopped fresh cilantro, divided use
I	17.3-ounce package frozen puff pastry (2 sheets), thawed for 30 minutes
1½	cups grated sharp Cheddar cheese, divided use

✳ In a small bowl stir together chili powder, brown sugar, pimenton, and salt. On a work surface sprinkled with 2 tablespoons cilantro, roll out I sheet puff pastry to a 12-inch square.

✳ Sprinkle square evenly with half of spice mixture and ¾ cup Cheddar, pressing cheese gently onto pastry. Roll up I edge to middle of pastry sheet and roll up parallel edge in same manner so that the 2 rolls are touching. Repeat procedure with remaining cilantro, pastry sheet, spice mixture, and Cheddar.

✳ Wrap pastry rolls in plastic wrap and chill 30 minutes. (Pastry rolls may be made 2 weeks ahead and frozen—let stand in refrigerator 2 hours before proceeding.)

✳ Preheat oven to 375°F.

✳ Cut pastry rolls with a sharp knife crosswise into slices just under ½-inch-thick and arrange I inch apart on large baking sheets. Bake palmiers in batches in middle of oven 18–20 minutes, or until golden brown, and transfer with a metal spatula to racks to cool. Makes about 48 palmiers.

✳ *Appetizers*

Parmesan-Sage Twists

These crispy, light and puffy appetizer twists are also delicious made with grated Romano or Manchego cheese.

1¾   cups finely grated Parmesan cheese
1½   teaspoons dried rubbed sage
½   teaspoon coarsely ground black pepper
½   of a 17.3-ounce package frozen puff pastry (1 sheet), thawed for 30 minutes

✳ In a small bowl mix the Parmesan cheese, sage, and pepper.

✳ Roll out puff pastry on lightly floured work surface into a 18x10-inch rectangle (pastry will be thin). Sprinkle one-third of cheese mixture evenly over half of pastry. Fold plain half of pastry over cheese, forming 10x9-inch rectangle; press to adhere. Repeat 2 more times, rolling to a 18x10-inch rectangle, sprinkling with one-third of cheese mixture and folding. Roll out pastry again into a 18x10-inch rectangle. Transfer to unlined baking sheet. Chill 30 minutes.

✳ Position 1 rack in top third and 1 rack in bottom third of oven; preheat to 425°F. Line 2 large baking sheets with parchment paper. Cut pastry crosswise in half, forming two 10x9-inch rectangles. Trim and discard uneven edges of pastry. Cut each rectangle crosswise into ½-inch-wide strips. Twist each strip a few times and place on prepared baking sheets, spacing ½ inch to ¾ inch apart, dabbing ends lightly with water and pressing to adhere to parchment.

✳ Bake twists until golden brown, reversing position of sheets halfway through baking, about 10 minutes total. Cool twists on sheets. Serve warm or at room temperature. Makes about 36 twists.

✔ **Cook's Note:** *Twists can be prepared 1 day ahead. Cover twists on sheets tightly with foil and store at room temperature. If desired, rewarm, uncovered, in 350°F oven until heated through, about 5 minutes.*

Appetizers ✳

Petite Pissaladières

Pissaladière is the south of France's answer to pizza. Here the flaky, pizza-like tart is prepared finger-size and loaded with traditional toppings.

½   of a 17.3-ounce package frozen puff pastry (1 sheet), thawed for 30 minutes

3   tablespoons olive oil, divided use

1   large onion, halved lengthwise and cut crosswise into ⅛-inch-thick slices

½   teaspoon salt

¼   teaspoon black pepper

3–4   flat anchovy fillets, patted dry and finely chopped

2   teaspoons chopped fresh thyme, divided use

¼   cup Kalamata or other brine-cured black olives, pitted and very thinly sliced lengthwise

✳ Preheat oven to 400°F.

✳ Roll out puff pastry on a lightly floured surface into a 12½-inch square, then trim edges to form a 12-inch square. Prick sheet all over with a fork. Cut into thirty-six (36) 2-inch squares and transfer to 2 large buttered baking sheets, arranging about 2 inches apart.

✳ Bake squares in upper and lower thirds of oven, switching position of pans halfway through baking, until puffed and golden, 12–15 minutes total. Transfer squares to a rack and cool until just warm.

✳ While pastry is baking, heat 2 tablespoons oil in a 12-inch nonstick skillet over moderate heat until hot but not smoking, then cook onion with salt and pepper, stirring occasionally, until golden brown, 15–18 minutes. Stir in anchovies (to taste) and 1 teaspoon thyme and keep warm, covered.

✳ Lightly brush tops of pastry squares with remaining tablespoon olive oil. Make a small indentation in center of each square with your finger, then top each with 1 teaspoon onion mixture and a few olive slivers. Sprinkle squares with remaining teaspoon thyme. Serve warm. Makes 36 tartlets.

✔ **Cook's Notes:** ✳ *Pastry squares can be baked 1 day ahead, cooled completely, and kept in an airtight container at room temperature. Reheat in a 350°F oven 6 minutes before topping.* ✳ *The onion mixture can be made 1 day ahead and chilled, covered. Reheat over moderate heat, stirring, until heated through, about 10 minutes.*

Appetizers

PETITE PISSALADIÈRES

Red Pepper & Boursin Tartlets

The Boursin in this recipe—a smooth, white, triple-cream cheese with a buttery texture, flavored with herbs and garlic—nearly melts into the crisp puff pastry once the tartlets are baked. In other words, heavenly.

1   17.3-ounce package frozen puff pastry (2 sheets), thawed for 30 minutes
⅓   cup herbed Boursin cheese, softened
2   whole roasted bell peppers (from a 7-ounce jar), drained, patted dry, and sliced into thin strips
2   teaspoons fresh thyme leaves (or 1 teaspoon dried thyme)
⅛   teaspoon kosher salt
    Pepper, to taste

* Preheat oven to 450°F.

* Unfold pastry sheets on a lightly floured surface and cut out an 8-inch round from each.

* Transfer rounds to a large nonstick baking sheet and prick all over with a fork, leaving a ½-inch border around edges.

* Spread the cheese evenly over each round, then scatter with peppers and sprinkle with thyme, kosher salt, and pepper to taste.

* Bake tarts in middle of oven until puffed and golden brown, about 15 minutes, then transfer to a rack to cool slightly. Cut each tart into 8 wedges and serve warm. Makes 16 hors d'oeuvres.

✔ **Cook's Note:** *Tarts can be assembled (but not baked) 1 day ahead and chilled, covered.*

Tuna & Olive Empanaditas

Pimento-stuffed green olives and jarred capers add a rich, salty note to these tender, hand-held tapas.

1	6-ounce can light tuna in olive oil (not drained)
$\frac{1}{2}$	cup finely chopped onion
$\frac{1}{2}$	cup finely chopped pimiento-stuffed green olives
2	tablespoons drained capers, rinsed and chopped
	Salt and pepper, to taste
1	17.3-ounce package frozen puff pastry (2 sheets), thawed for 30 minutes

✳ Preheat oven to 400°F.

✳ Pour oil from tuna into a medium skillet. Add onion to skillet and cook over moderate heat, stirring occasionally, until softened, about 3–4 minutes.

✳ Mash tuna in a bowl with a fork, then stir in onion, olives, and capers. Season generously with pepper and very lightly with salt.

✳ Roll out 1 pastry sheet on a lightly floured surface with a lightly floured rolling pin to a 13-inch square. Cut out 20 rounds with a small floured cookie cutter and discard trimmings. Repeat with second pastry sheet.

✳ Put a heaping teaspoon of the tuna mixture in center of each round. Hold 1 filled round in palm of your hand, then moisten edge with a finger dipped in water. Cup hand, then fold dough over to form a half-moon, pinching edges to seal.

✳ Transfer pastries to an ungreased large baking sheet and press back of a fork onto border to crimp. Form more empanaditas with remaining rounds, then bake on sheet in middle of oven until golden, 20–25 minutes. Cool empanaditas on baking sheet on a rack about 10 minutes. Serve warm. Makes about 40 hors d'oeuvres.

✔ **Cook's Note:** *Empanaditas can be formed (but not baked) and frozen 1 week ahead. Freeze in 1 layer in a shallow baking pan, then transfer to sealed plastic bags and keep frozen. Bake frozen empanaditas about 30 minutes.*

Appetizers
TUNA & OLIVE EMPANADITAS

Salami Spinwheels

Boldly seasoned salami finds perfect balance with puff pastry in these very pretty appetizer twirls. They're always a hit, no matter what the occasion.

½	cup grated Parmesan cheese
¾	teaspoon dried basil
¾	teaspoon dried oregano
¼	teaspoon ground black pepper
½	of a 17.3-ounce package frozen puff pastry (1 sheet), thawed for 30 minutes
2	tablespoons honey-Dijon mustard
2	ounces packaged thinly sliced salami
1	large egg, beaten to blend

＊ In a medium bowl mix the Parmesan cheese, basil, oregano, and pepper. Cut puff pastry crosswise in half to form 2 rectangles. Spread 1 tablespoon mustard over 1 puff pastry rectangle, leaving 1-inch plain border at 1 long edge.

＊ Place half of salami in single layer atop mustard. Top salami with half of cheese mixture. Brush plain border with egg. Starting at side opposite plain border, roll up pastry, sealing at egg-coated edge. Transfer pastry roll, seam side down, to medium baking sheet. Repeat with remaining pastry rectangle, mustard, salami, cheese mixture, and egg. Chill rolls until firm, about 30 minutes, or wrap and chill up to 1 day.

＊ Preheat oven to 400°F. Line 2 baking sheets with parchment paper. Cut each pastry roll into about thirty (30) ¼-inch-thick rounds. Transfer rounds to prepared sheets. Bake until golden, about 15 minutes. Transfer to platter; serve. Makes about 60 spinwheels.

Appetizers ＊

SALAMI SPINWHEELS

Spring Artichoke Tartlets

Inexpensive and flavorful, jarred marinated artichoke hearts become even more enticing when paired with fresh cherry tomatoes and topped with thyme-scented sour cream.

½	of a 17.3-ounce package frozen puff pastry (1 sheet), thawed for 30 minutes
2	large egg yolks, beaten lightly
½	cup sour cream
1	tablespoon chopped fresh thyme leaves
	Salt and pepper, to taste
2	cups quartered, drained marinated artichoke hearts (about 3 small jars)
20	vine-ripened cherry tomatoes, halved

✳ Preheat oven to 400° F and lightly flour a baking sheet.

✳ Unfold pastry on lightly floured surface and cut into 6 squares.

✳ In a bowl whisk together egg yolks, sour cream, thyme, and salt and pepper to taste. Arrange pastry squares on baking sheet and spoon one-fourth of mixture onto center of each. Top mixture with artichokes and tomatoes. Spoon remaining sour cream mixture over vegetables.

✳ Bake tarts in middle of oven until pastry is golden, about 12–14 minutes. Serve warm or at room temperature. Makes 6 tarts.

Appetizers

SPRING ARTICHOKE TARTLETS

Italian Sausage Rolls

Consider this the king of all appetizers. No matter what the occasion—from a formal cocktail party to a children's birthday party—they will be demolished in minutes. Perhaps it's because they taste like mini sausage-stuffed pizzas, all neatly bundled in petite packages of flaky puff pastry.

¼	cup fresh white breadcrumbs
2	tablespoons milk
½	pound sweet Italian sausages, casings removed
½	medium onion, finely chopped
2	large eggs, divided use
1	large garlic clove, finely chopped
1½	teaspoons dried oregano
	Salt and pepper, to taste
½	of a 17.3-ounce package frozen puff pastry (1 sheet), thawed for 30 minutes
1	cup purchased marinara sauce, heated

✳ Line a large baking sheet with parchment paper. In a small bowl combine the breadcrumbs and milk. Let stand until milk is absorbed, about 5 minutes. Transfer to food processor. Add sausages, onion, 1 egg, garlic, and oregano. Using on/off turns, process until blended. Season with salt and pepper.

✳ Lightly beat remaining egg in a small cup. Unfold pastry sheet on a lightly floured work surface. Roll out to a 12x10-inch rectangle. Cut pastry crosswise into three (3) 10x4-inch strips. Brush each strip with beaten egg.

✳ Spoon one-third of sausage mixture in narrow strip lengthwise down center of each pastry strip. Fold long sides in, covering filling and overlapping slightly in center; press seam to seal. Arrange rolls seam side down on prepared sheet. Cover and chill until rolls are firm, at least 30 minutes and up to 1 hour.

✳ Preheat oven to 425° F. Cut each roll crosswise into 8 pieces. Separate pieces on baking sheet. Brush with some of remaining beaten egg. Bake until rolls are puffed and golden, about 20 minutes. Serve warm with marinara sauce. Makes 24 rolls.

Appetizers ✳

Sherried Mushroom Empanadas

Mushrooms, sherry, and ham come together to capture the essence of Seville in these delicate puff pastry packages.

2	medium onions, finely chopped
6	tablespoons (¾ stick) unsalted butter
1½	pounds mushrooms, finely chopped
1	medium red bell pepper, finely chopped
1	cup finely chopped ham
⅓	cup cream sherry
1½	tablespoons chopped fresh oregano or 2 teaspoons dried oregano
3	tablespoons dry breadcrumbs
1	17.3-ounce package frozen puff pastry (2 sheets), thawed for 30 minutes
	An egg wash made by beating 1 large egg with 1 teaspoon water
	Salt and pepper, to taste

✳ In a large heavy skillet cook onions in butter over moderately low heat, stirring occasionally, until softened. Stir in mushrooms and bell pepper and cook over moderate heat, stirring occasionally, until the liquid the mushrooms give off is evaporated and mixture begins to brown. Add ham and sherry and cook, stirring, until liquid is evaporated.

✳ In a bowl stir together mushroom mixture, oregano, breadcrumbs, and salt and pepper to taste. Cool, uncovered, to room temperature.

✳ Preheat oven to 400°F.

✳ On a lightly floured surface roll out 1 pastry sheet to a 14 x 10-inch rectangle. Halve rectangle lengthwise with a long sharp knife and spread about half of mushroom filling on 1 half, leaving a 1-inch border all around. Brush edges of mushroom-topped pastry with some egg wash and put remaining pastry half on top of filling. Crimp edges of dough together with fork tines and cut several slits in empanada with a small sharp knife.

✳ Carefully transfer empanada with 2 spatulas to a large baking sheet, leaving room for second empanada, and brush with some remaining egg wash. Make another empanada in same manner with remaining pastry sheet, filling, and egg wash.

✳ Put empanadas in middle of oven and reduce temperature to 375°F. Bake empanadas until golden, about 35 minutes. With a serrated knife cut empanadas into ¾-inch slices. Makes 8–10 appetizer servings.

Appetizers

Dried Cherry & Almond Baked Brie

Baked, puff pastry-wrapped brie is a classic appetizer. The additions of tart-sweet dried cherries, delicately sweet almonds, and a hint of brown sugar lend style and flavor to this newfangled interpretation.

1	8-inch round (16 ounces) Brie cheese
¼	cup dried cherries
¼	cup sliced almonds, lightly toasted
3	tablespoons brown sugar
1	17.3-ounce package frozen puff pastry (2 sheets), thawed for 30 minutes
2	large eggs, beaten
	Pear slices, for serving
	Assorted crackers, for serving

✳ Preheat the oven to 400°F.

✳ Using a sharp knife, cut the wheel of brie in half horizontally and separate the top half of the wheel from the bottom half. Sprinkle the bottom half of the brie with the dried cherries, toasted almonds, and brown sugar.

✳ Replace the top half of the Brie and press down to secure the stuffing. On a lightly floured surface roll out the puff pastry to a 12-inch square. Place the brie in the middle of the puff pastry and fold the excess pastry around the wheel. Unfold the second piece of puff pastry and cut out decorations with cookie cutters or a sharp knife.

✳ Using a pastry brush, brush the beaten egg over the puff pastry-wrapped brie. Place the decorations on top of the brie; brush with more egg wash. Place the brie on a baking sheet lined with parchment paper.

✳ Bake for 20 minutes or until the pastry begins to turn pale golden brown. Reduce oven temperature to 325°F and bake for another 18–20 minutes until deep golden brown. Serve warm, with fruit and crackers. Makes 8–10 appetizer servings.

✔ **Cook's Note:** *The brie wheel can be stuffed, wrapped securely, and stored in the freezer up to a month ahead of time.*

Appetizers ✳

Roasted Pepper & Prosciutto Pinwheels

Fun and flavorful, these rolled-up appetizers are particularly handy for parties because they are easy to assemble ahead of time. Got a larger crowd? Just double the recipe.

½   of a 17.3-ounce package frozen puff pastry (1 sheet), thawed for 30 minutes
1   large egg, lightly beaten
2   ounces thinly sliced prosciutto
1   jarred roasted red pepper (from a 7-ounce jar), sliced 1-inch thick

✳ On a lightly floured surface arrange pastry sheet with a short side facing you and cut in half crosswise.

✳ Arrange half of the sheet with a long side facing you and brush edge of far side with some beaten egg. Arrange half of the prosciutto evenly on top of pastry, avoiding egg-brushed edge. Lay half of the pepper strips lengthwise along side of pastry facing you.

✳ Starting with side nearest you, roll pastry jelly roll–fashion and wrap in waxed paper. Make another log in same manner with remaining puff pastry, prosciutto, pepper, and egg.

✳ Chill pastry logs, seam sides down, until firm, at least 30 minutes.

✳ Cut logs crosswise into ½-inch-thick pinwheels and arrange, cut sides down, 1 inch apart on baking sheets lined with parchment paper.

✳ Preheat oven to 400°F. Bake pinwheels in batches in middle of oven until golden, about 14–16 minutes. Transfer pinwheels to a rack and cool slightly. Makes about 28 appetizers.

✳*Appetizers*

You just can't go wrong with these scrumptious sausage puffs. Chicken-apple sausage is merely one option for the filling—any other variety of fully cooked link sausage will do.

I	17.3-ounce package frozen puff pastry (2 sheets), thawed for 30 minutes
3	tablespoons honey mustard
4	chicken apple sausages, each cut crosswise into 3 pieces

✳ Preheat the oven to 350°F. On a lightly floured surface, cut each puff pastry sheet into six (6) 2x4-inch rectangles.

✳ Spread each piece of puff pastry with honey mustard. Wrap one piece of sausage inside each piece of puff pastry. Press seam to seal.

✳ Place pastries, seam-side down, on a nonstick baking sheet. Place in the oven and bake until the puff pastry is golden brown, about 12–15 minutes. Serve warm. Makes 12 appetizers.

Mini-Cheeseburger Pastry Bundles

Petite burgers get jazzed up with melted cheese and puff pastry to create an appetizer everyone will adore. Vary the cheese and ground meat in a multitude of ways for ever-new, go-to hors d'oeuvres.

1¼	pounds lean ground beef
1	tablespoon steak sauce
1	teaspoon season salt
¼	teaspoon freshly ground black pepper
½	cup minced green onions
1	17.3-ounce package frozen puff pastry (2 sheets), thawed for 30 minutes
12	1-inch square slices Havarti or Cheddar cheese (about ¼-inch-thick slices)

✳ In a medium bowl combine the ground beef, steak sauce, salt, black pepper, and chopped green onions until blended. Hand-form meat into 12 patties, about 2 inches in diameter. In large nonstick skillet set over medium-high heat, cook burgers to medium, turning once (be careful not to overcook). Cool to room temperature.

✳ Preheat oven to 350°F.

✳ Roll out 1 puff pastry sheet on a lightly floured surface to a 10-inch square. Cut into 6 rectangles. Repeat with second puff pastry sheet. Place one burger in center of each puff pastry rectangle and top with a slice of cheese. Fold edges up and twist on top.

✳ Place pastries on a nonstick cookie sheet and bake 20–25 minutes until golden brown. Serve warm. Makes 12 mini-burgers.

✔ **Cook's Note:** *The burger bundles can be prepared up to a day in advance. Refrigerate, loosely covered with plastic wrap, until ready to bake.*

✳ *Appetizers*

Spicy Beef Samosas

Just the right amount of spices and herbs makes these samosas—triangular, east-Indian pastries—deliciously robust. Although traditional samosas are deep fried, I think you'll agree that this puff pastry variation is every bit as delicious.

1	medium onion, minced
½	of a medium green bell pepper, seeded and finely chopped
1	pound extra-lean ground beef
2	teaspoons curry powder
½	teaspoon each: ground cumin, salt, and black pepper
2	tablespoons olive oil
½	cup water
1	hard boiled large egg, finely chopped
⅓	cup golden raisins, finely chopped
2	tablespoons chopped fresh mint
1	17.3-ounce package frozen puff pastry (2 sheets), thawed for 30 minutes
1	large egg, lightly beaten

✳ In a large nonstick skillet sauté onion, bell pepper, ground beef, curry powder, cumin, salt, and pepper in olive oil until lightly browned. Add water and simmer covered until meat is cooked through. Remove from heat and let cool. Fold in the chopped boiled egg, chopped raisins, and mint.

✳ Preheat oven to 375°F.

✳ Roll out 1 puff pastry sheet on a lightly floured surface to a 14x10-inch rectangle. Cut pastry with either a fluted dough press or cookie cutter to make eight (8) 3½-inch circles. Repeat with second sheet of puff pastry.

✳ While holding 1 circle at a time in your hand, spoon 1 teaspoon of meat mixture into the middle. Fold pastry in half and secure the circle by pressing the edges together with a fork to make a seal. Repeat with remaining ingredients.

✳ Place the samosas on a baking sheet lined with parchment paper; brush the tops with egg. Bake for about 20–22 minutes or until pastry is well puffed and golden. Remove from the oven, let cool then serve. Makes 16 samosas.

Golden Onion Tartlets

One bite of these buttery onion and goat cheese morsels and you may think you've been transported to the South of France.

2	tablespoons butter
2	cups thinly sliced onions (about 2 medium onions)
	Salt and pepper, to taste
2	cloves garlic, minced
4	ounces goat cheese, crumbled
I	17.3-ounce package frozen puff pastry (2 sheets), thawed for 30 minutes
I	large egg, lightly beaten
2	tablespoons chopped fresh chives

✱ Line a baking sheet with parchment paper. In a medium skillet set over medium heat melt the butter. Add the onions. Season with salt and pepper. Sauté until the onions start to wilt, about 4 minutes.

✱ Stir in the garlic and continue to cook for 1 minute. Remove from the heat and cool completely. In a medium mixing bowl combine the onions and cheese. Mix well. Season with salt and pepper.

✱ Preheat the oven to 375°F.

✱ Roll out 1 puff pastry sheet on a lightly floured surface to a 12 x 10-inch rectangle. Cut pastry with either a fluted dough press or cookie cutter to make twelve (12) 2½-inch circles. Repeat with second sheet of puff pastry.

✱ Place rounds on the parchment-lined baking sheet, prick each round randomly with the tines of a fork, and brush with the beaten egg. Spread a tablespoon of the onion mixture on each round, leaving a ⅛-inch border.

✱ Bake until lightly browned, about 14–17 minutes. Remove from the oven and sprinkle with the chives. Serve warm. Makes 24 tartlets.

Appetizers

GOLDEN ONION TARTLETS

Cheese Straws with Variations

While testing this recipe, I was torn as to which variation I liked best—plain, with pesto, spicy, or seeded. In the end, I decided to include the variations and let you decide for yourself. You won't be disappointed, no matter which flavor direction you choose.

1	17.3-ounce package frozen puff pastry (2 sheets), thawed for 30 minutes
1	large egg
1	tablespoon water
¼	cup grated Parmesan cheese
¼	cup grated white Cheddar cheese
	Salt and pepper, to taste
	Optional flavorings: prepared pesto sauce, cayenne pepper, sesame seeds

✳ Preheat the oven to 400°F.

✳ Roll out 1 puff pastry sheet on a lightly floured surface to a 12 x 18-inch rectangle. Repeat with second sheet of puff pastry.

✳ In a small bowl beat together the egg and water to make an egg wash.

✳ Lightly brush one of the pastry sheets with the egg wash. Sprinkle with the cheeses and season with salt and pepper to taste. Top with the remaining sheet of pastry, pressing firmly to adhere, then lightly roll with the rolling pin. With a knife, trim the edges to make even. (If desired, change the flavor of the straws by using pesto sauce instead of the egg wash, top with the cheese, and proceed as directed. Or sprinkle with cayenne or sesame seeds.)

✳ Cut the dough crosswise into individual strips, about ⅓ to ½-inch wide. Twist each 3 times to make a spiral and place on an ungreased baking sheet. Bake until golden brown, about 18–20 minutes.

✳ Remove and transfer to a serving platter. Serve warm or room temperature. Makes about 36 cheese straws.

Appetizers ✳

Shrimp and Romano Crisps

Served with glasses of full-bodied wine, these warm shrimp and cheese bites make for an appetizer extraordinaire.

½   of a 17.3-ounce package frozen puff pastry (1 sheet), thawed for 30 minutes

1   6-ounce can tiny shrimp, well drained, divided use

½   cup jarred sundried tomato tapenade

⅔   cup finely shredded Romano cheese

10   grape or cherry tomatoes, halved

✳ Preheat oven to 375°F.

✳ Unfold pastry. Using a 1½-inch fluted or round cutter, cut pastry into about 20 circles. Do not re-roll pastry scraps. Place pastry rounds on an ungreased baking sheet. Bake about 14–16 minutes or until puffed and lightly browned. Remove to a wire rack and let cool.

✳ Reserve 20 of the shrimp; set aside. Split pastry rounds. Evenly spread ½ teaspoon of the tomato tapenade over the bottom half of each round. Top with some of the remaining shrimp. Sprinkle with cheese. Replace tops. Return filled pastries to baking sheet.

✳ Bake about 5–8 minutes more or until cheese is just melted. Serve warm. Garnish each serving with a tomato half and a shrimp. Makes about 20 appetizers.

Appetizers

Artichoke-Parmesan Mini-Crescents

Parmesan cheese is always wonderful sprinkled over a big bowl of spaghetti, but its rich flavor is capable of so much more, as these scrumptious appetizers illustrate. The ingredients are all pantry items, meaning you can assemble these on the spur of the moment.

¾	cup chopped frozen (thawed) artichoke hearts
⅓	cup plain dry breadcrumbs
½	cup freshly grated Parmesan cheese
¼	cup chopped fresh parsley
2	large eggs, divided use
I	clove garlic, minced
¼	teaspoon salt
⅛	teaspoon freshly ground pepper
2	I7.3-ounce packages frozen puff pastry (4 sheets), thawed for 30 minutes

✳ Preheat oven to 425°F. In a small bowl combine the artichokes, breadcrumbs, Parmesan, parsley, I of the eggs, garlic, salt, and pepper.

✳ On a lightly floured surface roll out I of the puff pastry sheets to an I8 x I0-inch rectangle. With a 2½-inch round biscuit cutter, cut out I8 circles. Repeat with second puff pastry sheet.

✳ Beat the remaining egg and brush over circles. Refrigerate I0 minutes. Spoon I rounded teaspoon filling on each circle and fold dough over filling then press edges to seal.

✳ Brush tops of crescents with beaten egg and transfer to a baking sheet lined with parchment paper. Bake about I4–I7 minutes or until puffed and browned. Serve warm. Makes 36 crescents.

✔ **Cook's Note:** *To make ahead, bake the crescents and let cool on a wire rack, then wrap well in plastic wrap and foil and freeze up to I month. Reheat in a 400°F oven about I5 minutes.*

Seeded Spice Sticks

The combination of black and white sesame seeds makes for very dramatic, and very addictive, appetizers. Feel free to experiment with different varieties of seeds and spices to create your own unique treat.

1	large egg yolk
1	teaspoon water
1	17.3-ounce package frozen puff pastry (2 sheets), thawed for 30 minutes
1	teaspoon cumin seeds, crushed
1	teaspoon salt
1	tablespoon white sesame seeds
1	tablespoon black sesame seeds

✳ Preheat oven to 400°F.

✳ Beat yolk with water in a small cup.

✳ Roll out 1 pastry sheet to a 12 x 16-inch rectangle on a lightly floured board. Brush with yolk mixture. Sprinkle with half the cumin, half the salt, half the white sesame seeds, and half the black sesame seeds. Roll top lightly with rolling pin; let stand 5 minutes.

✳ Turn pastry over, seed-side down, and brush top with yolk mixture. Fold in half crosswise. Roll into a 10 x 16-inch rectangle. Cut along the 10-inch side into ¾-inch-wide strips. Twist strips; arrange 1 inch apart on an ungreased cookie sheet.

✳ Bake 10–12 minutes, until golden. Repeat with remaining puff pastry, seeds and salt. Makes 24 seed sticks.

Appetizers

Shrimp and Bacon Napoleons

With a hint of Dijon mustard, layers of light pastry, and the mingling flavors of shrimp and bacon, this all-American, yet newly styled napoleon isn't missing a thing.

I   17.3-ounce package frozen puff pastry (2 sheets), thawed for 30 minutes

2   3-ounce packages cream cheese, softened

I   tablespoon Dijon-style mustard

I   tablespoon white wine Worcestershire sauce

I   tablespoon thinly sliced green onion

2½   cups chopped, cooked, peeled, and deveined shrimp (about 18 ounces uncooked)

⅓   cup shredded carrot

⅓   cup crumbled crisp-cooked bacon (about 4 slices)

✳ Preheat oven to 425°F. Line two large baking sheets with parchment paper.

✳ Unfold one sheet of puff pastry on a lightly floured surface. Using a pastry wheel or a sharp knife, cut sheet into 9 squares (about 3x3 inches each); cut each square in half to make a total of 18 rectangles. Place rectangles about 1 inch apart on prepared baking sheets.

✳ Bake in preheated oven for 12–15 minutes or until golden. Carefully remove from baking sheet; cool on a wire rack. Repeat with remaining sheet of puff pastry.

✳ For filling, combine cream cheese, mustard, Worcestershire sauce, and green onion. Fold in cooked shrimp, carrot, and bacon. To assemble, use tines of a fork to separate each pastry in half horizontally. Spread a rounded tablespoon of filling on the bottom portion of each pastry; replace top layer. Makes 36 appetizers.

Roasted Pepper Ricotta Puffs

Layered with flavor from sweet ricotta cheese and jarred roasted peppers, these divine morsels will garner heaps of praise from the guests who are lucky enough to get a sample.

1	17.3-ounce package frozen puff pastry (2 sheets), thawed for 30 minutes
½	cup ricotta cheese
½	cup chopped jarred roasted red sweet pepper
5	tablespoons grated Romano cheese, divided use
1	tablespoon snipped fresh parsley
1	teaspoon dried oregano, crushed
½	teaspoon ground black pepper
1	large egg, lightly beaten

✳ Unfold the pastry on a lightly floured surface. Using a sharp knife, cut each pastry sheet into nine (9) 3-inch squares.

✳ In a medium bowl stir together the ricotta cheese, roasted red pepper, 3 tablespoons Romano cheese, parsley, oregano, and black pepper.

✳ Brush the edges of each pastry square with beaten egg. Spoon about 2 teaspoons filling onto one half of each pastry square. Fold the other half of the pastry over the filling, forming a rectangle. Seal edges by pressing with the tines of a fork. With a sharp knife, cut slits in the top of each pastry bundle. Brush with egg; sprinkle with some of the remaining 2 tablespoons Romano cheese.

✳ Arrange pastry bundles on a baking sheet lined with parchment paper. Chill 30 minutes.

✳ Preheat oven to 400°F. Bake pastries 18–20 minutes or until golden brown. Transfer to a wire rack; cool for 5 minutes before serving. Makes 18 puffs.

✳ *Appetizers*

Provencal Tapenade Tartlets

½ of a 17.3-ounce package frozen puff pastry (1 sheet), thawed for 30 minutes

⅓ cup jarred olive tapenade

8 cherry tomatoes, quartered

½ of an 8-ounce package crumbled feta cheese

Fresh herb sprigs (optional)

✳ Preheat oven to 425°F. Unfold puff pastry onto a lightly floured cutting board. Cut into sixteen (16) 2½-inch squares.

✳ Place each square in a mini muffin cup. Place about 1 teaspoon of the tapenade on each square. Top with two cherry tomato quarters and some of the feta cheese.

✳ Bake 12–15 minutes or until pastry is puffed and golden brown. Remove from muffin cups. Garnish with fresh herb sprigs, if desired. Serve warm. Makes 16 tartlets.

Ratatouille Napoleons

Ratatouille, a popular mixed vegetable and herb dish from Provence, reaches new heights of elegance in this tiered napoleon appetizer.

2	tablespoons olive oil
1½	cups chopped, peeled eggplant
1½	cups coarsely chopped zucchini
½	cup chopped onion
1	14.5-ounce can diced tomatoes with basil, oregano, and garlic
½	cup finely chopped cooked ham
¼	teaspoon ground black pepper
1	17.3-ounce package frozen puff pastry (2 sheets), thawed for 30 minutes
1	large egg
1	tablespoon water

✳ For ratatouille, heat the olive oil in a large skillet and cook the eggplant, zucchini, and onion about 5 minutes or until onion is tender, stirring occasionally. Stir in tomatoes; bring to boiling. Reduce heat and simmer, uncovered, for 5 minutes or until most of liquid has evaporated. Stir in ham and pepper. Cool to room temperature.

✳ Unfold pastry on a lightly floured surface. Trim a very thin strip from each side using a long knife. Cut each sheet into three strips along fold lines; cut each strip crosswise into five rectangles, making 30 total. Place 24 of the rectangles on ungreased baking sheets. Combine egg and water; brush mixture on rectangles. Cut each of the remaining rectangles into 8 strips each (48 strips total; strips may be cut crosswise or lengthwise with a pastry wheel, if desired). Crisscross each pastry rectangle with 2 strips. Brush strips with egg mixture.

✳ Preheat oven to 400°F. Bake 14–17 minutes or until golden. Transfer to wire racks and cool. Split pastries in half horizontally. Place baked sides down on baking sheets; bake 3 minutes longer. Cool on wire racks.

✳ To serve, place bottom halves of rectangles on serving platter. Spoon about 2 tablespoons of the ratatouille mixture on each. Add tops. Makes 24.

✔ **Cook's Note:** *The unfilled, baked pastries may be frozen in sealed containers up to 3 months. Another make-ahead option is to prepare the ratatouille ahead and chill it up to 3 days. Once assembled, the napoleons will hold up to 1 hour.*

✳ *Appetizers*

Crab Melt Pastries with Fresh Lime

Lime makes this easy crab appetizer pop, especially when combined with a few spoonfuls of sharp mustard—each flavor amps up the other.

3	6-ounce cans crabmeat, drained
1½	tablespoons fresh lime juice
1	teaspoon grated lime zest
2	tablespoons mayonnaise
2	teaspoons coarse-grained or Dijon mustard
	Salt and pepper, to taste
⅔	cup shredded Swiss cheese
½	of a 17.3-ounce package frozen puff pastry (1 sheet), thawed for 30 minutes
1	large egg yolk, beaten

✳ Preheat oven to 400°F.

✳ In a medium bowl combine the crabmeat, lime juice, lime zest, mayonnaise, and mustard. Season to taste with salt & pepper. Mix in the cheese.

✳ On a lightly floured surface roll out pastry sheet to a 14x9-inch rectangle. Cut into 6 equal squares.

✳ Spoon crab mixture down centers of squares to within ½ inch of ends. Fold two sides of each square in half over filling to form a rectangle. Seal ends and seams well.

✳ Place seam side down on an ungreased baking sheet. Brush with egg yolk. Bake 15–18 minutes or until golden brown. Remove from oven. Serve warm or at room temperature. Makes 6 servings.

Texas Chicken Empanadas

Good to the last bite, these Texas-spiced, standout tapas are sure to turn heads at your next party.

2½	cups chopped, cooked chicken
½	cup grated Pepper Jack cheese
½	cup thick and chunky-style salsa
2	tablespoons chopped fresh cilantro leaves
I	teaspoon ground cumin
2	tablespoons sour cream
I	tablespoon seeded and finely chopped jalapeño pepper
I½	17.3-ounce packages frozen puff pastry (3 sheets), thawed for 30 minutes
I	large egg
I	tablespoon water

✳ Preheat oven to 400°F.

✳ In a medium bowl combine chicken, Pepper Jack cheese, salsa, cilantro, cumin, sour cream, and jalapeño until blended.

✳ Place a sheet of puff pastry on a lightly floured surface. Roll out to a 13-inch square. With a 3-inch round cutter, cut pastry into 16 rounds. Place a generous teaspoon of chicken mixture slightly off center on each round. Brush edges of pastry circles with cold water. Fold circles over filling into half-moon shapes. Pinch edges with fingers or a fork to seal tightly. Prick with a fork.

✳ Place on a lightly greased baking sheet. In a small bowl mix the egg and water with a fork; brush over the empanadas. Repeat with the remaining pastry and filling.

✳ Bake empanadas 12–15 minutes or until golden brown. Serve warm. Makes 48 empanadas.

✳ *Appetizers*

Herbed Mushroom Envelopes

Enhanced with thyme, sage, and a touch of butter, these deeply flavored morsels of goodness are worth making time and again.

I	tablespoon butter
I	medium onion, chopped
½	pound button mushrooms, finely chopped
I	clove garlic, minced
I	teaspoon salt
½	teaspoon dried thyme
¼	teaspoon ground black pepper
¼	teaspoon dried rubbed sage
½	cup dry white wine
½	of a 17.3-ounce package frozen puff pastry (I sheet), thawed for 30 minutes
I	large egg, lightly beaten

✳ Melt butter in large skillet over medium heat. Add onion; cook 2 minutes or until softened. Add mushrooms and garlic; sauté 3 minutes until mushrooms release liquid. Add salt, thyme, pepper, and sage; sauté I minute. Add wine; simmer 15–20 minutes or until all liquid has been absorbed. Cool.

✳ Preheat oven to 400°F.

✳ Meanwhile, roll out pastry on lightly floured surface to a 12½-inch square. Neatly trim to 12-inch square. Cut sheet into sixteen (16) 3-inch squares.

✳ Brush each square with a little egg. Spoon I slightly rounded tablespoon filling in center of each square. Fold each square of pastry in half diagonally into a triangle, bringing one corner to opposite corner. Gently pinch edges together to seal, making sure all the filling is sealed inside. With tines of fork, press edges together to seal. Cut a few small slashes in top of each turnover. Brush each turnover with some of the egg.

✳ Bake for 14–17 minutes or until puffed and golden. Serve warm or room temperature. Makes 16 turnovers.

✔ **Cook's Note:** *If you wish, before baking, turnovers may be refrigerated several hours or frozen up to 2 weeks. Thaw before baking.*

Appetizers

Sausage-Stuffed Tomatoes in Puff Pastry

Rich, flavorful sausage adds heft to these summery tomato appetizers.

6	small vine-ripened tomatoes
	Salt, to taste
½	of a 17.3-ounce package frozen puff pastry (1 sheet), thawed for 30 minutes
1	tablespoon olive oil
1	small onion, coarsely chopped
⅓	cup very thinly sliced celery
8	ounces sweet Italian sausage, casings removed, crumbled
2	tablespoons finely chopped fresh flat-leaf parsley
½	cup finely grated Parmesan cheese
1	large egg
1	tablespoon heavy cream

❋ Cut tops off tomatoes and reserve. Scoop out and discard seeds; sprinkle insides of tomatoes with salt. Drain upside down on a rack set over a baking sheet. Meanwhile, roll out puff pastry to a 13 x 12-inch rectangle on lightly floured surface; cut into 6 rectangles. Press into cups of a standard muffin tin, overhanging sides. Cover with plastic wrap and refrigerate.

❋ Heat oil in a nonstick skillet over medium-high heat until hot but not smoking. Add onion and celery; cook until onion is golden, about 3 minutes. Add sausage; cook, stirring occasionally, until browned, about 10 minutes. Remove from heat; stir in parsley and Parmesan cheese.

❋ Preheat oven to 400°F.

❋ Divide sausage mixture among tomatoes; place 1 in each pastry shell. Lightly beat egg with cream; brush onto edges of shells. Turn corners of pastry up around tomato slightly.

❋ Bake until pastry is golden, about 14–17 minutes; return tomato tops halfway through baking. Let rest 10 minutes before serving. Makes 6 servings.

Appetizers

Caviar Pillows

Gorgeous, easy to make, and utterly sublime—what more could you ask of an appetizer?

½	of a 17.3-ounce package frozen puff pastry (1 sheet), thawed for 30 minutes
1	large egg
1	tablespoon water
1	4-ounce container whipped chive cream cheese
	About half of a 2-ounce jar salmon caviar
	About half of a 2-ounce jar black lumpfish caviar
	Small parsley leaves for garnish

✳ On lightly floured surface, with floured rolling pin, roll out puff pastry sheet to a 10-inch square. With fluted pastry wheel or knife, cut pastry into 4 strips; cut each strip crosswise into 4 pieces; cut each piece diagonally in half to make 32 triangles.

✳ Preheat oven to 375°F. Arrange triangles ½ inch apart on large cookie sheet. Press 1-inch round cookie or biscuit cutter into center of each triangle almost but not all the way through. In cup, beat egg with water. Brush triangles with egg mixture.

✳ Bake triangles 14–17 minutes or until puffed and golden. Transfer to wire racks to cool.

✳ With small knife, cut out circle in center of each puff-pastry triangle. Spoon whipped cream cheese into small pastry bag with ¼-inch writing tube. Pipe some whipped cream cheese into hole in each triangle. Top 16 of the pastries with ¼ teaspoon salmon caviar (red) and 16 with lumpfish caviar. Garnish each with small parsley leaf. Makes 32 hors d'oeuvres.

Cheese & Ham Spirals

This is your go-to appetizer for a wide range of occasions. Delicious made with the ham and Parmesan combination I've given here, you can vary the types of cheese and deli meats to suit your tastes or to what you happen to have on hand.

1	large egg
1	tablespoon water
½	of a 17.3-ounce package frozen puff pastry (1 sheet), thawed for 30 minutes
¼	cup grated Parmesan cheese, divided use
¼	teaspoon cayenne pepper
8	slices very thinly sliced deli ham

✱ Preheat oven to 400°F. In a small cup beat egg and water with fork until blended; set aside.

✱ Unfold pastry on lightly floured surface. Roll out to a 14x10-inch rectangle; cut in half lengthwise. Brush both pastry halves lightly with some of the egg mixture. Sprinkle 3 tablespoons of the cheese and the pepper evenly over 1 of the pastry pieces; cover with ham slices. Place remaining pastry piece, egg side down, over ham. Brush with additional egg mixture. Roll gently with rolling pin to seal.

✱ Roll jelly roll–fashion to make 14-inch log. Cut into 24 equal slices. Place, cut side down, on parchment-covered baking sheet. Brush with remaining egg mixture; sprinkle with remaining tablespoon cheese.

✱ Bake 12–14 minutes or until golden brown. Serve warm or at room temperature. Makes 24 appetizers.

✔ **Cook's Note:** *To make ahead, prepare as directed except for baking. Wrap securely; freeze. When ready to serve, defrost; slice and bake as directed.*

✱ *Appetizers*

Creamy Crab-Stuffed Pastry Bites

Make your next social gathering special with these bite-sized treats. Golden layers of puffed pastry add effortless elegance to these creamy crab hors d'oeuvres.

4	ounces (half of an 8-ounce package) cream cheese, softened
½	cup well-drained canned crab (from a 6-ounce can)
2	green onions, chopped
2	teaspoons dried tarragon
	Salt and pepper, to taste
1	17.3-ounce package frozen puff pastry (2 sheets), thawed for 30 minutes
1	large egg
1	tablespoon milk

✱ Preheat oven to 400°F.

✱ In a small bowl mix cream cheese, crab, onions, and tarragon until well blended. Season with salt and pepper to taste.

✱ Place pastry sheets on a lightly floured cutting board. Roll out to a 14 x 10-inch rectangle. Cut out 22 circles from each pastry sheet, using a 2-inch round cutter. In a small cup beat egg and milk with fork until well blended.

✱ Spoon 1 teaspoon of the crab mixture onto center of each pastry circle. Brush edge of pastry with egg mixture. Fold pastry in half to completely enclose filling; press edges together to seal. Place on baking sheet; brush tops with remaining egg mixture.

✱ Bake 12–15 minutes or until golden brown. Serve immediately. Makes 44 appetizers.

✔ **Cook's Note:** *To make ahead, assemble appetizers as directed but do not brush with egg mixture. Place in a freezer-weight resealable plastic bag. Remove excess air from bag and seal. Freeze up to 3 months. When ready to serve, remove appetizers from freezer and place in a single layer on baking sheet. Brush with egg mixture. Bake at 400°F for 15–17 minutes or until heated through and golden brown.*

Appetizers

Wasabi Shrimp Puffs

Wasabi is a bright green-colored condiment that is the Japanese version of horseradish. Its sharp, pungent, fiery flavor adds just the right kick to these scrumptious, sushi-inspired shrimp bites.

2	6-ounce cans tiny shrimp, drained and chopped
½	cup mayonnaise
½	cup finely chopped green onion
2	tablespoons chopped drained pickled ginger
2½	teaspoons wasabi powder
1	17.3-ounce package frozen puff pastry (2 sheets), thawed for 30 minutes
1	large egg white, lightly beaten
2	tablespoons sesame seeds

✳ Preheat oven to 350°F. In a small bowl mix shrimp, mayonnaise, green onion, pickled ginger, and wasabi; cover. Refrigerate until ready to serve.

✳ Unfold pastry sheets onto baking sheets; brush evenly with egg white. Sprinkle with sesame seeds. Cut each sheet into eighteen (18) 3 x 1½-inch rectangles. Do not separate rectangles.

✳ Bake 22–25 minutes until puffed and golden. Remove pastry from baking sheets; cool completely. Separate pastry into rectangles. Split each rectangle horizontally in half. Spoon 1 tablespoon of the shrimp mixture onto bottom half of each rectangle; cover with top of rectangle. Serve warm. Makes 36 appetizers.

Appetizers

Club Sandwich Petites

The timeless triple-decker deli sandwich gets new life in this irresistible, bite-sized appetizer.

I	17.3-ounce package frozen puff pastry (2 sheets), thawed for 30 minutes
I	8-ounce container chive cream cheese spread
I	cup grated Swiss cheese
½	cup chopped smoked deli turkey
⅓	cup chopped red pepper
I	large egg, lightly beaten
2	tablespoons Dijon mustard
2	tablespoons real bacon bits
¼	cup chopped chives (optional)

✳ Preheat oven to 425°F.

✳ Roll out each pastry sheet to a 12x9-inch rectangle on lightly floured surface; cut each rectangle into twelve (12) 3-inch squares. Place I pastry square, with pastry corners pointing up, in each of 24 medium muffin cups.

✳ In a medium bowl mix the cream cheese spread, Swiss cheese, turkey, red pepper, egg, Dijon mustard, and bacon until well blended. Spoon I tablespoon of the cheese mixture into each pastry cup.

✳ Bake 15–18 minutes or until filling is heated through and pastry is golden brown. If desired, sprinkle each cup with chopped chives. Makes 24 pastry cups.

Cranberry & Blue Cheese Triangles

This is a case of assertive opposites finding delicious balance.

3	tablespoons butter
1	tablespoon olive oil
4	sweet (e.g., Vidalia) onions (about 2 pounds total), peeled and very thinly sliced
1	firm-ripe pear, rinsed and cut in half crosswise, then lengthwise Salt and pepper, to taste
1	17.3-ounce package frozen puff pastry (2 sheets), thawed for 30 minutes
⅓	cup chopped dried cranberries
7	ounces (about 1½ cups) crumbled Gorgonzola or other blue cheese

* In a 12-inch skillet set over medium heat melt the butter with the olive oil. Add the sliced onions and reduce heat slightly (between medium and medium-low). Cook, stirring occasionally, until the onions soften and turn brown, about 30–35 minutes. Meanwhile, trim the pear quarters to remove seeds, then cut into thin slices; set aside. When onions are done, sprinkle with salt and pepper to taste and set aside to cool to room temperature.

* Preheat oven to 375°F. Line two baking sheets with parchment paper. Transfer one sheet of pastry to each. Roll out pastry lightly with a floured rolling pin to flatten any creases.

* Using a pizza cutter or sharp knife, cut the pastry sheets into triangle, wedge, or diamond-shaped pieces about 2 inches wide. Slightly separate pieces so that they are not touching.

* Sprinkle 1 teaspoon chopped cranberries in the center of each wedge. Top with a small pile of caramelized onions and about ½ teaspoon of the Gorgonzola or blue cheese.

* Bake in oven until fully puffed and golden, about 25–30 minutes. Serve warm. Makes about 40 appetizers.

✔ **Cook's Note:** *To make ahead, cook the onions up to 2 days ahead and store in an airtight container in the refrigerator.*

Appetizers

Salmon-Tarragon Mini Turnovers

Petite bites of refinement, these appetizers are surprisingly simple to prepare from readily available pantry ingredients. Fresh lemon zest, parsley, and tarragon add bright notes of flavor to the sour-cream-enriched salmon filling.

½	cup sour cream
1	teaspoon grated lemon zest
½	teaspoon salt
½	teaspoon fresh-ground pepper
2	tablespoons chopped fresh parsley
1	tablespoon chopped fresh tarragon
1	14-ounce can salmon, drained
1	17.3-ounce packages frozen puff pastry (2 sheets), thawed for 30 minutes
1	large egg, beaten to blend with 1 tablespoon water

✳ Preheat oven to 400°F.

✳ In a large bowl combine the sour cream, lemon zest, salt, pepper, parsley, and tarragon. Mix in the drained salmon; set aside.

✳ Cut each puff pastry sheet into nine (9) 3-inch squares. On a lightly floured work surface, with a lightly floured rolling pin, roll each square once in each direction to flatten and stretch to approximately 4 inches. Place 1 tablespoon filling in the middle of each square. Brush edges lightly with egg mixture and fold diagonally over filling to make triangles; pinch edges to seal.

✳ Arrange pastries ½ inch apart on two baking sheets lined with parchment paper. Lightly brush the top of each pastry with egg mixture.

✳ Bake pastries 20–25 minutes until golden brown. Serve warm or at room temperature. Makes 18 pastries.

Minted Lamb Puff Pastry Bites

These seasonally inspired hors d'oeuvres are sure to make a dazzling impression.

- ¾   pound ground lamb
- 2   green onions, finely chopped
- ⅓   cup minced fresh mint
- 3   garlic cloves, pressed
       Salt and pepper, to taste
- ½   of a 17.3-ounce package frozen puff pastry (1 sheet), thawed for 30 minutes
- 1   large egg, lightly beaten
       Plain yogurt, mango chutney, or both (optional)

✳ In a medium bowl mix the lamb, green onions, mint, garlic, salt, and pepper.

✳ Unfold pastry sheet on floured work surface. Roll out to a 12x10-inch rectangle. Cut pastry crosswise into three (3) 10x4-inch strips. Brush each strip with beaten egg. Spoon one-third of lamb mixture in narrow strip lengthwise down center of each pastry strip. Fold long sides in, covering filling and overlapping slightly in center; press seam to seal.

✳ Arrange rolls seam-side down on prepared sheet. Cover and chill until rolls are firm, at least 30 minutes and up to 1 hour.

✳ Preheat oven to 425° F. Line a baking sheet with parchment paper. Cut each roll crosswise into 8 pieces. Separate pieces on baking sheet. Brush with some of remaining beaten egg. Bake until rolls are puffed and golden, about 20 minutes. Serve warm with yogurt, chutney, or both. Makes 24 rolls.

✳ *Appetizers*

Chorizo Empanaditas

Be sure to select fresh chorizo (Mexican style) for these spicy tapas, as opposed to Spanish-style chorizo, which is similar to salami and other cooked, cured sausages.

12	ounces bulk fresh chorizo or other spicy sausage
½	cup chopped onion
½	cup chopped green bell pepper
2	large garlic cloves, minced
½	cup chopped seeded tomato
I	tablespoon chopped fresh oregano leaves or 1½ teaspoons dried
I	17.3-ounce package frozen puff pastry (2 sheets), thawed for 30 minutes

✳ In a large skillet set over medium-high heat cook sausage, onion, bell pepper, and garlic, stirring occasionally, until sausage is browned and onion is softened, about 5–6 minutes. Drain well. Stir in tomato and oregano. Cool to room temperature.

✳ Preheat oven to 400°F.

✳ On a lightly floured surface roll out I sheet puff pastry to a 12-inch square. Cut into 16 3-inch squares. Place I rounded tablespoon filling in center of each square. Fold opposite corners of squares together to form triangles. Pinch edges of pastry together; crimp with fork to seal. Place triangles onto ungreased baking sheets. Repeat with remaining pastry sheet and filling.

✳ Bake 18–20 minutes or until golden brown. Cool. Serve warm or at room temperature. Makes 32 appetizers.

✔ **Cook's Note:** *Empanadas can be made ahead. Cover and refrigerate for up to 6 hours or wrap and freeze for up to 1 month.*

Bite-Size Calzones

A classic trio of Italian ingredients—sausage, marinara sauce, and cheese—makes one great appetizer. Or pile a few on a plate, serve up some salad, and you have dinner.

½ pound Italian sausage, casings removed

½ cup finely chopped red bell pepper

¼ cup finely chopped fresh flat leaf parsley

3 tablespoons jarred marinara sauce

1 17.3-ounce package frozen puff pastry (2 sheets), thawed for 30 minutes

½ cup shredded Italian blend cheese or mozzarella

2 tablespoons olive oil

Additional marinara sauce, warmed (optional)

✳ Cook sausage and pepper in large skillet over medium heat, stirring occasionally to break up sausage, until cooked through, about 6–8 minutes. Remove from heat; stir in parsley and marinara sauce. Cool to room temperature.

✳ Preheat oven to 400°F.

✳ On a lightly floured surface roll out 1 sheet puff pastry into a 14-inch square. Cut into sixteen (16) 3½-inch squares. Place 1 tablespoon filling and 1 teaspoon cheese in center of each square. Lightly brush edges of square with water. Fold opposite corners of squares together to form triangles; crimp with fork to seal. Place onto ungreased baking sheet. Repeat with remaining pastry sheet and filling.

✳ Lightly brush each calzone with olive oil. Bake for 10–12 minutes or until puffed and lightly browned. Serve immediately. Serve with additional warmed marinara sauce, if desired. Makes 32 appetizers.

✔ **Cook's Note:** *To make ahead, wrap unbaked calzones in plastic food wrap. Place in refrigerator for up to 24 hours. When ready to serve, bake as directed above.*

Appetizers

Vegetable Samosas

Lend some exotic flair to your next get-together with these scrumptious samosas. Inspired by traditional Indian street food, this puff pastry variation is far easier to prepare, and much lighter, than its deep-fried cousins.

1	15-ounce can whole or sliced potatoes, drained
2½	teaspoons curry powder
1	cup frozen peas, thawed
3	tablespoons minced fresh cilantro
5	tablespoons vegetable oil, divided use
½	cup chopped onion
1	large carrot, peeled and coarsely grated
	Salt and freshly ground pepper, to taste
1	17.3-ounce package frozen puff pastry (2 sheets), thawed for 30 minutes
1	large egg
1	tablespoon water
2	teaspoons caraway seeds

✳ Place the drained potatoes, curry powder, peas, cilantro, and 2 tablespoons of the oil in a medium bowl. Coarsely mash with a fork. Set aside.

✳ In a sauté pan over medium heat, warm the remaining 3 tablespoons oil. Add the onion and sauté until softened, 3–4 minutes. Add the carrot and sauté until the carrot has softened, 3–4 minutes longer. Stir the onion and carrot into the potatoes. Mix well and season with salt and pepper. Set aside to cool.

✳ On a lightly floured surface roll out 1 sheet puff pastry to a 14-inch square. Cut into sixteen (16) 3½-inch squares. In a small cup mix the egg and water. Place about 1 tablespoon of the potato mixture in the center of each round. Brush the edges of the round with some of the egg-water mixture, fold in half, and press the edges together to seal. Repeat with remaining pastry and filling.

✳ Place the filled pastries on a baking sheet lined with parchment paper; brush with the remaining egg-water mixture. Sprinkle the tops with the caraway seeds. Cover and refrigerate for 30 minutes.

✳ Preheat an oven to 400°F. Bake the samosas until golden brown, about 15–18 minutes. Serve warm. Makes about 32 samosas.

Appetizers ✳

Apricot, Pecan & Brie Tartlets

The cheese and dessert course never tasted so good. These divine little bites are extremely well-suited for everything from bridal showers to formal cocktail parties.

24	pecan halves
1	8-ounce round of Brie, chilled
½	of a 17.3-ounce package frozen puff pastry (1 sheet), thawed for 30 minutes
⅓	cup apricot preserves

✳ Toast pecans at 350°F in a shallow pan for 10 minutes until golden and fragrant; cool.

✳ Increase oven temperature to 425°F.

✳ Cut rind off of cheese. Cut cheese into 24 cubes; set aside.

✳ Roll out pastry to a 15x10-inch rectangle on a lightly floured surface. Cut into 24 squares. Fit squares into miniature muffin pans, extending corners slightly above cup rims.

✳ Bake pastry for 10–12 minutes or until it begins to brown. Remove from oven and gently press handle of a wooden spoon into center of each pastry, forming tart shells.

✳ Spoon ½ teaspoon preserves into each shell; top with a cheese cube and a pecan half. Bake 5 more minutes or until cheese melts; serve immediately. Makes 2 dozen tartlets.

✳ Appetizers

APRICOT, PECAN & BRIE TARTLETS

Provencal Elephant Ears

A good quality extra-virgin olive oil makes all the difference here. It adds a mellow, grassy flavor to these very French, double-spiral appetizers.

1	17.3-ounce package frozen puff pastry (2 sheets), thawed for 30 minutes
¼	cup extra-virgin olive oil
2	garlic cloves, minced
½	teaspoon salt
3	tablespoons minced shallots
2	tablespoons chopped Kalamata or other brine-cured olives
2	tablespoons chopped dried tomatoes packed in oil
1	tablespoon minced fresh parsley
1	large egg yolk
1	tablespoon water

✳ On a lightly floured surface roll out 1 pastry sheet to a 13 x 11-inch rectangle. In a small bowl stir together olive oil, garlic, and salt. Brush half of olive oil mixture over pastry. Sprinkle with half each of the shallots, olives, dried tomatoes, and minced parsley.

✳ Roll up pastry, jelly roll–fashion, starting with each short side and ending at middle of pastry sheet. Repeat procedure with remaining pastry sheet, olive oil mixture, shallots, olives, tomatoes, and parsley. Loosely wrap rolls in plastic wrap and refrigerate at least 30 minutes.

✳ Preheat oven to 400°F. Cut rolls crosswise into ⅓-inch-thick slices. Place on baking sheets lined with parchment paper.

✳ Whisk together egg yolk and 1 tablespoon water and brush evenly over pastries.

✳ Bake 10–12 minutes or until golden brown. Makes about 5 dozen appetizers.

Portobello Mushroom Napoleon Appetizers

Not your typical first-course fare, this whimsical take on napoleons breathes fresh air and plenty of style into a classic preparation.

½	of a 17.3-ounce package frozen puff pastry (1 sheet), thawed for 30 minutes
8	ounces portobello mushrooms
2	tablespoons butter
3	tablespoons chopped fresh basil
9	slices deli provolone cheese, cut in half
4	Roma tomatoes, thinly sliced

❋ Preheat oven to 400°F.

❋ Unfold pastry on lightly floured surface. Cut into 3 strips along fold marks. Cut each strip into 6 rectangles. Place 2 inches apart on baking sheet.

❋ Bake 14–17 minutes or until golden. Remove from baking sheet and cool on wire rack. Keep oven on.

❋ Remove stems from mushrooms and discard. Cut mushroom caps into ½-inch slices. In a medium skillet set over medium-high heat, melt the butter. Add mushrooms and cook until tender and liquid evaporates. Stir in basil.

❋ Split pastries into 2 layers, making 36 layers in all. Place 18 bottom layers on baking sheet. Loosely roll cheese. Divide tomatoes, mushrooms, and cheese among bottom layers. Top with top layers.

❋ Bake for 5 minutes or until cheese melts. Serve warm. Makes 18 napoleons.

❋ *Appetizers*

Pot Pies, Pizzas, Quiche & Other Entrées

Smoky Southwest Pizza

It's been decades since pizza has been considered exotic. Now we think of it as down-home, all-American fare of the best kind. This version maintains its homey provenance with a Southwestern twist.

2	teaspoons yellow cornmeal
½	of a 17.3-ounce package frozen puff pastry (1 sheet), thawed for 30 minutes
1½	cups purchased thick & chunky chipotle salsa
2	tablespoons olive oil
1½	teaspoons chili powder
1½	cups shredded Mexican-style four-cheese mix
¼	cup chopped fresh cilantro

✳ Line a baking sheet with parchment paper; sprinkle with cornmeal. On a lightly floured surface unfold pastry sheet and gently roll out to a 14 x 12-inch rectangle. Transfer pastry to baking sheet and prick all over with a fork. Chill pastry, covered, at least 30 minutes and up to 1 day.

✳ Preheat oven to 400°F.

✳ In a small bowl mix salsa, oil, and chili powder. In a medium bowl toss the cheese and cilantro.

✳ Bake pastry in middle of oven 15 minutes until light golden. Spoon salsa mixture over dough, leaving ½-inch border. Sprinkle with cheese mixture. Bake pizza until crust is golden brown and cheese is melted and bubbling, about 10 minutes. Cut into squares and serve. Makes 4 servings.

Pizza Bianca with Prosciutto, Arugula & Parmesan

The salty-sweet flavor of prosciutto, the fresh bite of arugula, and the rich, sharp nuttiness of Parmesan—all are anchored by delicate layers of puff pastry in this very sophisticated interpretation of pizza.

½   of a 17.3-ounce package frozen puff pastry (1 sheet), thawed for 30 minutes

4   tablespoons extra-virgin olive oil, divided use

1   cup (packed) arugula leaves

8   thin slices prosciutto

1   4-ounce piece Parmesan cheese, shaved with a vegetable peeler

     Salt and pepper, to taste

✳ Line a baking sheet with parchment paper. On a lightly floured surface unfold pastry sheet and gently roll out to a 14x12-inch rectangle. Transfer pastry to baking sheet and prick all over with a fork. Chill pastry, covered, at least 30 minutes and up to 1 day.

✳ Preheat oven to 400°F.

✳ Drizzle puff pastry with 2 tablespoons olive oil. Bake pastry in middle of oven until deep golden, about 18–20 minutes.

✳ Layer the arugula, prosciutto slices, and Parmesan cheese over the puff pastry. Season with salt and pepper.

✳ Bake pizza 5 minutes longer until cheese is just beginning to melt. Cut into squares and serve, drizzling each piece with ½ tablespoon of the remaining olive oil. Makes 4 servings.

Tomato-Pesto Pizza

You're only four ingredients away from a terrific supper. Sweet tomatoes and purchased pesto combine in this streamlined, but oh-so-appealing, take on the classic pizza pie.

½	of a 17.3-ounce package frozen puff pastry (1 sheet), thawed for 30 minutes
¼	cup purchased basil pesto
1½	cups shredded mozzarella
3	Roma tomatoes, cut crosswise into ⅛-inch slices
	Salt and pepper, to taste

✳ Line a baking sheet with parchment paper. On a lightly floured surface unfold pastry sheet and gently roll out to a 14 x 12-inch rectangle. Transfer pastry to baking sheet and prick all over with a fork. Chill pastry, covered, at least 30 minutes and up to 1 day.

✳ Preheat oven to 400°F.

✳ Bake pastry in middle of oven 15 minutes until light golden.

✳ Spread pesto over pastry leaving a 1-inch border. Sprinkle with cheese. Arrange tomato slices over cheese and season with salt and pepper.

✳ Bake pizza until crust is golden brown and cheese is melted and bubbling, about 10 minutes. Cut into squares and serve. Makes 4 servings.

Reuben Pizza

Here the Reuben sandwich, a New York deli mainstay made from layers of corned beef, Swiss cheese, and sauerkraut, is enlightened as a quick and easy pizza. The result? Pizza supreme.

½ of a 17.3-ounce package frozen puff pastry (1 sheet), thawed for 30 minutes

1 tablespoon olive oil

1 large onion, sliced

1 teaspoon caraway seeds

1 cup (packed) well-drained sauerkraut from jar
   Freshly ground pepper, to taste

3 tablespoons Dijon mustard

1½ cups shredded Swiss cheese

8 ounces fully cooked kielbasa sausage, thinly sliced into rounds
   Salt and pepper, to taste

❋ Line a baking sheet with parchment paper. On a lightly floured surface unfold pastry sheet and gently roll out to a 14 x 12-inch rectangle. Transfer pastry to baking sheet and prick all over with a fork. Chill pastry, covered, at least 30 minutes and up to 1 day.

❋ Preheat oven to 400°F.

❋ In large heavy skillet over medium-high heat, heat the oil. Add onion and caraway seeds and sauté until onion just begins to brown, about 7 minutes. Transfer onion mixture to large bowl. Mix in sauerkraut. Cool to lukewarm. Season generously with pepper.

❋ Bake pastry in middle of oven 15 minutes until light golden.

❋ Spread mustard over pastry leaving a 1-inch border. Sprinkle with cheese. Arrange sausage slices over cheese and season with salt and pepper.

❋ Bake pizza until crust is golden brown and cheese is melted and bubbling, about 10 minutes. Cut into squares and serve. Makes 4 servings.

Pot Pies, Pizza, Quiche & Other Entrées

Smoked Salmon Pizza

High-quality ingredients transform this humble pizza into an extremely satisfying, and sophisticated, supper. Alternatively, cut the pizza into slender wedges and serve as an appetizer.

- ½ of a 17.3-ounce package frozen puff pastry (1 sheet), thawed for 30 minutes
- ½ cup ricotta cheese
- 3 tablespoons purchased pesto
- 3 tablespoons pine nuts
- 3 ounces thinly sliced smoked salmon, cut into 1-inch pieces
- Fresh basil sprigs

✳ Line a baking sheet with parchment paper. On a lightly floured surface unfold pastry sheet and gently roll out to a 14x12-inch rectangle. Transfer pastry to baking sheet and prick all over with a fork. Chill pastry, covered, at least 30 minutes and up to 1 day.

✳ Preheat oven to 400°F.

✳ Blend cheese and pesto in small bowl.

✳ Bake pastry in middle of oven 15 minutes until light golden.

✳ Spread ricotta mixture over pastry leaving a 1-inch border. Bake 10 minutes. Sprinkle with pine nuts. Bake pizza until crust is set and golden, about 5–8 minutes longer.

✳ Arrange smoked salmon over pizza. Garnish with basil and serve. Cut into squares and serve. Makes 4 servings.

Wild Mushroom–Sausage Pizza

Among the many wonderful things about this pizza are that it cooks quickly and is substantial without being heavy, making it the perfect transition dinner from winter to spring.

½ of a 17.3-ounce package frozen puff pastry (I sheet), thawed for 30 minutes

2 tablespoons olive oil, divided use

½ pound bulk Italian sausage

I small red onion, thinly sliced

½ pound fresh wild mushrooms (such as stemmed shiitake, oyster, or chanterelle), thickly sliced

I teaspoon finely chopped fresh rosemary

Salt and pepper, to taste

1¾ cups grated mozzarella cheese

Chopped fresh parsley (optional)

✳ Line a baking sheet with parchment paper. On a lightly floured surface unfold pastry sheet and gently roll out to a 14x12-inch rectangle. Transfer pastry to baking sheet and prick all over with a fork. Chill pastry, covered, at least 30 minutes and up to I day.

✳ Preheat oven to 400°F.

✳ Heat I tablespoon olive oil in large nonstick skillet over medium-high heat. Add sausage. Sauté until brown, breaking into ½-inch pieces with back of spoon, about 5 minutes. Using slotted spoon, transfer sausage to bowl. Add onion to skillet. Sauté until crisp-tender, about 2 minutes; transfer to plate.

✳ Add remaining I tablespoon oil to skillet. Add mushrooms and rosemary; sprinkle with salt and pepper. Sauté until brown, about 5 minutes.

✳ Bake pastry in middle of oven 15 minutes until light golden.

✳ Layer sausage, onion, and mushrooms over pastry leaving a I-inch border. Sprinkle with cheese. Bake pizza until crust is golden brown and cheese is melted and bubbling, about 10 minutes. If desired, sprinkle with parsley. Cut into squares and serve. Makes 4 servings.

Pot Pies, Pizza, Quiche & Other Entrées

BBQ Chicken Pizza

With barbecue sauce, chicken, cilantro, and Pepper Jack cheese, this puffed-up pizza takes a delectable Southern detour.

½	of a 17.3-ounce package frozen puff pastry (1 sheet), thawed for 30 minutes
1½	cups grated Pepper Jack cheese
6	tablespoons chopped fresh cilantro, divided use
6	tablespoons purchased barbecue sauce, divided use
2	cups cooked shredded or cubed chicken
1	small red onion, very thinly sliced

✳ Line a baking sheet with parchment paper. On a lightly floured surface unfold pastry sheet and gently roll out to a 14x12-inch rectangle. Transfer pastry to baking sheet and prick all over with a fork. Chill pastry, covered, at least 30 minutes and up to 1 day.

✳ Preheat oven to 400°F. Bake pastry in middle of oven 15 minutes until light golden.

✳ In a small bowl mix the cheese and 4 tablespoons cilantro.

✳ Spread 4 tablespoons barbecue sauce over pastry leaving a 1-inch border. Layer with chicken. Drizzle remaining 2 tablespoons sauce over chicken. Sprinkle with cheese mixture and arrange onion slices on top of cheese.

✳ Bake pizza until crust is golden brown and cheese is melted and bubbling, about 10 minutes. Cut into squares, sprinkle with remaining 2 tablespoons cilantro and serve. Makes 4 servings.

Greek Feta & Artichoke Pizza

Here pizza goes Greek with the big bright flavors of fresh mint, feta cheese, sweet onions, and ripe tomatoes.

½	of a 17.3-ounce package frozen puff pastry (1 sheet), thawed for 30 minutes
1	6.5-ounce jar marinated artichoke hearts, drained, 2 tablespoons marinade reserved
1	tablespoon yellow cornmeal
6	ounces Roma tomatoes, thinly sliced into rounds
4	ounces crumbled herb-seasoned feta cheese
½	medium-size sweet onion (such as Vidalia or Maui), thinly sliced
2	tablespoons thinly sliced fresh mint

✳ Line a baking sheet with parchment paper. On a lightly floured surface unfold pastry sheet and gently roll out to a 14x12-inch rectangle. Transfer pastry to baking sheet and prick all over with a fork. Chill pastry, covered, at least 30 minutes and up to 1 day.

✳ Preheat oven to 400°F.

✳ Cut artichokes into ½-inch pieces.

✳ Bake pastry in middle of oven 15 minutes until light golden.

✳ Top pastry with artichokes, tomato slices, cheese, and sweet onion slices. Drizzle with the reserved artichoke marinade.

✳ Bake pizza until crust is crisp and golden, about 12 minutes. Transfer to platter. Sprinkle with mint. Cut pizza into 4 squares and serve. Makes 4 servings.

Deluxe Vegetarian Pizza

Check the salad bar at the supermarket for an assortment of pre-sliced and pre-chopped vegetables. The convenience will save both time and money because you can purchase small amounts of exactly what you need and want to top this delicious pizza.

½	of a 17.3-ounce package frozen puff pastry (1 sheet), thawed for 30 minutes
3	tablespoons olive oil
1⅓	cups shredded Monterey Jack cheese
4	ounces crumbled goat cheese (or feta cheese)
1½	cups sliced mushrooms
½	cup finely chopped red onion
1	cup diced green bell pepper
1	cup diced seeded plum tomatoes
½	cup minced pitted Kalamata olives
	Salt and pepper, to taste

✳ Line a baking sheet with parchment paper. On a lightly floured surface unfold pastry sheet and gently roll out to a 14x12-inch rectangle. Transfer pastry to baking sheet and prick all over with a fork. Chill pastry, covered, at least 30 minutes and up to 1 day.

✳ Preheat oven to 400°F.

✳ Bake pastry in middle of oven 15 minutes until light golden.

✳ Sprinkle with cheeses, mushrooms, onion, bell pepper, tomatoes, and olives. Sprinkle with salt and pepper.

✳ Bake pizza until crust is golden brown and cheese is melted and bubbling, about 12 minutes. Cut into squares and serve. Makes 4 servings.

Margarita Pizza

Here I've lightened traditional margarita pizza with a puffed pastry crust and fresh basil to achieve a bright, summertime flavor. It goes without saying that the better the tomatoes, the better the pizza.

½	of a 17.3-ounce package frozen puff pastry (1 sheet), thawed
1¾	cups grated mozzarella cheese
1	small red onion, very thinly sliced
1½	pounds Roma tomatoes, halved, seeded, sliced into rounds
⅓	cup grated Parmesan cheese
3	tablespoons sliced fresh basil

* Line a baking sheet with parchment paper. On a lightly floured surface unfold pastry sheet and gently roll out to a 14x12-inch rectangle. Transfer pastry to baking sheet and prick all over with a fork. Chill pastry, covered, at least 30 minutes and up to 1 day.

* Preheat oven to 400°F.

* Top pastry with even layers of mozzarella cheese and onion, then tomatoes. Sprinkle with Parmesan.

* Bake until crust is crisp and golden brown at edges, cheese melts, and tomatoes are tender, about 30 minutes. Let stand 5 minutes. Cut into 4 pieces, topping with fresh basil. Makes 4 servings.

Peach, Goat Cheese & Prosciutto Pizza

Although you can use frozen, thawed peaches in a pinch, this elegant pizza is simply extraordinary when prepared with the ripest, sweetest fresh peaches of summer.

½ of a 17.3-ounce package frozen puff pastry (1 sheet), thawed for 30 minutes

2 tablespoons extra-virgin olive oil

1½ firm-ripe peaches, cut into thin wedges and halved crosswise

8 very thin prosciutto slices, torn into pieces

4 ounces soft mild goat cheese, crumbled

2 teaspoons chopped fresh rosemary

Salt and pepper, to taste

✻ Line a baking sheet with parchment paper. On a lightly floured surface unfold pastry sheet and gently roll out to a 14x12-inch rectangle. Transfer pastry to baking sheet and prick all over with a fork. Chill pastry, covered, at least 30 minutes and up to 1 day.

✻ Preheat oven to 400°F.

✻ Brush puff pastry with olive oil. Bake pastry in middle of oven 13–15 minutes until light golden.

✻ Top pastry with the peaches, prosciutto, cheese, and rosemary. Season with salt and pepper.

✻ Bake pizza until crust is golden brown, about 10 minutes. Cut into squares and serve. Makes 4 servings.

Three-Cheese & Sage Pizza

The musky-mint flavor of sage is the impeccable complement to a blend of pleasantly nutty, melted cheeses in this sophisticated pizza.

½   of a 17.3-ounce package frozen puff pastry (1 sheet), thawed for 30 minutes

¾   cup finely diced Fontina cheese

¼   cup crumbled blue cheese

½   medium red onion, sliced thin into rings

6   large fresh sage leaves, halved, or 1 teaspoon dried sage, crumbled

¼   cup freshly grated Parmesan cheese

¼   teaspoon freshly cracked black pepper

✳ Line a baking sheet with parchment paper. On a lightly floured surface unfold pastry sheet and gently roll out to a 14x12-inch rectangle. Transfer pastry to baking sheet and prick all over with a fork. Chill pastry, covered, at least 30 minutes and up to 1 day.

✳ Preheat oven to 400°F.

✳ Bake pastry in middle of oven 15 minutes until light golden.

✳ Scatter the Fontina and the blue cheese evenly over the dough, leaving a ½-inch border. Arrange the onion rings and the fresh sage leaves over the cheese. Sprinkle the pizza with the Parmesan. Sprinkle with pepper.

✳ Bake pizza until crust is golden brown and cheese is melted and bubbling, about 12 minutes. Cut into squares and serve. Makes 4 servings.

✳ *Pot Pies, Pizza, Quiche & Other Entrées*

Classic Chicken Pot Pie

This is the superlative pot pie, hearty with chunks of chicken and vegetables, then refined with a delicate cream sauce and tender puff pastry topping.

½	of a 17.3-ounce package frozen puff pastry (1 sheet), thawed for 30 minutes
1	tablespoon butter
1	cup diced celery
⅓	cup finely chopped shallots
3	cups canned low-salt chicken broth
2	bay leaves
1	teaspoon dried thyme
1½	pounds skinless boneless chicken breast halves
1	cup whipping cream
1	10-ounce russet potato, peeled, cut into ½-inch cubes
1	cup frozen peas
	Salt and pepper, to taste

✳ Preheat oven to 375°F. Roll out pastry on lightly floured surface to a 13x9-inch rectangle. Transfer to a baking sheet and chill. Butter an 11x7-inch glass baking dish.

✳ Melt butter in large saucepan over medium-high heat. Add celery and shallots; sauté 5 minutes. Add broth, bay leaves, and thyme; bring to boil. Add chicken. Reduce heat to medium-low and simmer until chicken is just cooked through, about 12 minutes. Remove chicken and bay leaves.

✳ Increase heat to medium; boil mixture until reduced to 1½ cups, about 15 minutes. Add cream and return to boil. Add potato cubes; cover and cook until tender, about 10 minutes. Remove pan from heat. Cut chicken into bite-size chunks and add to pan. Mix in peas. Season with salt and pepper.

✳ Pour mixture into the buttered baking dish. Top with pastry; press overhang to sides of dish. Bake until golden, about 30–35 minutes. Makes 4–6 servings.

Country Sausage Breakfast Pot Pie

This stick-to-your-ribs breakfast for a crowd is ideal fare for holiday mornings or special weekends.

I	pound country-style breakfast sausage
I	large shallot, minced
½	pound fresh mushrooms, sliced
I	8-ounce package cream cheese, cut into small chunks
8	large eggs
¼	cup packaged unseasoned breadcrumbs
½	of a 17.3-ounce package frozen puff pastry (1 sheet), thawed for 30 minutes
2	tablespoons butter, melted

✳ Preheat oven to 350°F. In a large skillet set over medium-high heat, brown sausage, breaking up with the back of a wooden spoon, until cooked through. Remove from skillet to paper-towel-lined plate.

✳ Add shallot to skillet and sauté until softened, about 2 minutes. Add mushrooms and sauté until browned, about 6 minutes. Add cheese and sausage to skillet; cook, stirring, until cheese has melted, about 3 minutes. Spoon into ungreased 8x8x2-inch baking pan.

✳ In same skillet, scramble eggs, leaving slightly undercooked. Spoon eggs over sausage. Sprinkle with breadcrumbs.

✳ On a lightly floured surface roll out puff pastry to a 9-inch square. Brush with some melted butter. Place pastry on baking pan, butter side down; crimp edges. Brush with butter. Cut 5 steam vents.

✳ Bake 30–35 minutes until pastry is golden brown and filling is bubbly. Makes 6 servings.

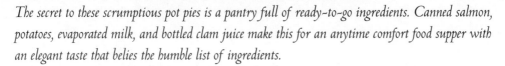

Salmon Pot Pies

The secret to these scrumptious pot pies is a pantry full of ready-to-go ingredients. Canned salmon, potatoes, evaporated milk, and bottled clam juice make this for an anytime comfort food supper with an elegant taste that belies the humble list of ingredients.

½	of a 17.3-ounce package frozen puff pastry (1 sheet), thawed for 30 minutes
1	12-ounce can evaporated milk
2	8-ounce bottles clam juice
3	tablespoons all-purpose flour
2	tablespoons butter, softened
¼	pound thickly sliced bacon, cut into ¼-inch cubes
1	medium onion, finely chopped
2	15-ounce cans of whole potatoes, drained and diced
3	tablespoons chopped fresh dill or 1 tablespoon dried dill
3	tablespoons chopped parsley
1½	tablespoons fresh lemon juice
1	teaspoon grated lemon zest
	Salt and pepper, to taste
2	14-ounce cans salmon, drained

✳ Preheat the oven to 375°F. Line a baking sheet with parchment paper.

✳ On a floured surface roll out the puff pastry to a 13 x 16-inch rectangle. Using a 5-inch plate, cut out 6 rounds. Transfer to the baking sheet. Bake for 15 minutes until puffed and golden. Cool.

✳ In a large saucepan combine the evaporated milk, clam juice, flour, and butter. Bring to a simmer and whisk until slightly thickened, about 6–7 minutes. Remove sauce from heat.

✳ In a large skillet, cook the bacon over low heat until crisp; transfer to a paper-towel-lined plate. Pour off all but 3 tablespoons of the fat. Add the onion and cook until softened.

✳ Stir the potatoes, bacon, onion, dill, parsley, lemon juice, and lemon zest into the sauce; season with salt and pepper to taste. Gently stir in the salmon and heat through, about 4–5 minutes. Spoon into 1¼-cup bowls, top with the pastry puffs and serve. Makes 6 servings.

Chipotle & Cheese Beef Pot Pie

A great supper option on a cold-weather night, this hearty beef and Cheddar pot pie gets a hint of heat and smoke from canned chipotle chile peppers packed in adobo sauce.

½ of a 17.3-ounce package frozen puff pastry (1 sheet), thawed for 30 minutes

2 tablespoons milk

½ cup shredded sharp Cheddar cheese

3 small zucchini, trimmed and cut into chunks

1 medium onion, coarsely chopped

1 teaspoon ground cumin

1 teaspoon olive oil

2 14.5-ounce cans stewed tomatoes with Mexican seasonings, undrained

1 14.5-ounce can yellow hominy, rinsed and drained

1 2-pound package cooked boned beef pot roast with gravy

2 canned chipotle chilies in adobo sauce, chopped, plus 1 teaspoon of the adobo sauce

2 tablespoons cornstarch

Salt and pepper

✳ Unfold pastry on a lightly floured board. If necessary, roll out or cut pastry to fit snugly inside top of a shallow 3-quart casserole (9 x 13 inches). Transfer pastry to a 12 x 15-inch nonstick baking sheet. Brush lightly with milk and sprinkle evenly with cheese. Cover with plastic wrap and freeze for 1 hour.

✳ Preheat oven to 425° F.

✳ Uncover pastry and bake until golden brown, 10–15 minutes.

✳ Meanwhile, in a 5- to 6-quart pan over high heat, sauté the zucchini, onion, and cumin in olive oil until vegetables are lightly browned, about 7–9 minutes. Add the tomatoes and their juices, and hominy; bring to a boil.

✳ Discard any fat from pot roast and sauce. Scrape gravy from beef and reserve. Cut beef into ¾-inch chunks.

✳ Add beef and gravy to pan and mix; cover and bring to a boil. Reduce heat to low and simmer, stirring occasionally, until beef is hot, 7–9 minutes. Add chiles and

Pot Pies, Pizza, Quiche & Other Entrées

adobo sauce. In a small bowl mix cornstarch and 3 tablespoons water. Add to pan and stir until boiling.

* Pour hot mixture into a warmed shallow casserole. Set hot pastry on filling. Use a large spoon to break through pastry and scoop out portions. Add salt and pepper to taste. Makes 8 servings.

Gumbo Pot Pies

Based on traditional gumbo—a Creole specialty and New Orleans mainstay—these puff pastry pot pies are surefire hits.

¼	cup all-purpose flour
¼	cup vegetable oil
1	medium-size green bell pepper, chopped
1	medium onion, chopped
2	garlic cloves, minced
1	pound fresh or frozen sliced okra
1	10-ounce can whole tomatoes with green chiles
1	teaspoon dried thyme
4–5	drops hot sauce, or to taste
¾	cup canned chicken broth
½	pound medium-size frozen, thawed shrimp, peeled and deveined
2	cups chopped, cooked chicken or turkey
½	of a 17.3-ounce package frozen puff pastry (1 sheet), thawed for 30 minutes
1	large egg, lightly beaten with a fork

✳ In a Dutch oven, whisk together all-purpose flour and vegetable oil; cook over medium heat, whisking constantly, 15–20 minutes or until roux is caramel colored. Stir in chopped bell pepper, onion, and garlic; cook 2 minutes. Add sliced okra, tomatoes and chiles, dried thyme, hot sauce, and chicken broth. Cover, reduce heat, and simmer 30 minutes.

✳ Add shrimp and chicken to gumbo; cook 8 minutes or just until shrimp turn pink. Remove from heat and cool slightly.

✳ Roll pastry sheet into an 11-inch square on a lightly floured surface; cut into four (4) 5-inch squares. Return pastry to freezer for at least 15 minutes. Cut out decorative shapes from excess pastry strips.

✳ Preheat oven to 400° F. Ladle gumbo into 4 ovenproof soup bowls, filling three-fourths full. Place 1 pastry square over each bowl, pressing firmly to sides to seal edges. Place decorative shapes on top of pastry. Brush pastry with beaten egg.

✳ Bake 18–22 minutes or until pastry is puffed and golden. Serve warm. Makes 4 servings.

Pot Pies, Pizza, Quiche & Other Entrées

Fresh Corn Quiche

This dish has a particularly lively, fresh taste, making it perfect for a late-summer supper when the fresh corn is bountiful and especially sweet.

½ of a 17.3-ounce package frozen puff pastry (1 sheet), thawed for 30 minutes

3 large eggs

¾ cup chopped onion

1 tablespoon all purpose flour

1 tablespoon sugar

1 tablespoon chopped fresh thyme or 1 teaspoon dried thyme

1 teaspoon salt

1⅓ cups half and half

3 tablespoons butter, melted

2 cups fresh corn kernels (cut from about 2 ears) or frozen, thawed

✳ Preheat oven to 375°F. Roll out puff pastry on a lightly floured surface to an 11-inch square. Transfer to 9-inch diameter glass pie plate. Trim edges. Place in refrigerator.

✳ In a blender or food processor combine the eggs, onion, flour, sugar, thyme, and salt. Blend until onion is almost smooth. Add half and half and butter; blend until smooth. Transfer to a large bowl and stir in the corn. Pour mixture into prepared crust.

✳ Bake until crust is golden brown and filling is set, about 42–45 minutes. Cool 15 minutes before serving. Makes 6 servings.

Arugula & Bacon Quiche

In this easy and hugely satisfying quiche, arugula is transformed from peppery salad leaf into a powerhouse pie ingredient. Bacon is the herb's heaven-made match.

½ of a 17.3-ounce package frozen puff pastry (1 sheet), thawed for 30 minutes

6 bacon slices, cut into ½-inch pieces

½ cup chopped shallots

5 cups fresh arugula, stems trimmed, leaves coarsely chopped

2 teaspoons balsamic vinegar

1 cup heavy whipping cream

3 large eggs

½ teaspoon salt

¼ teaspoon ground black pepper

1 cup grated Swiss cheese

✳ Preheat oven to 400°F. Roll out puff pastry on a lightly floured surface to an 11-inch square. Transfer to 9-inch diameter glass pie plate. Trim edges. Place in refrigerator.

✳ Cook bacon in large skillet over medium-high heat until crisp, about 5 minutes. Using slotted spoon, transfer to paper-towel-lined plate and drain. Add shallots to same skillet and sauté until tender, about 2 minutes. Add arugula and sauté until just wilted, about 1 minute. Remove from heat. Add balsamic vinegar; toss to combine.

✳ Sprinkle arugula mixture, then bacon over prepared crust. In a large bowl, whisk cream, eggs, salt, and pepper to blend. Stir in cheese. Pour mixture into crust.

✳ Bake quiche until filling is slightly puffed and golden, about 35–40 minutes. Let stand 10 minutes. Cut into wedges. Makes 6 servings.

✳ *Pot Pies, Pizza, Quiche & Other Entrées*

Chile Relleno Quiche

In this recipe, canned green chiles taste as good as fresh, thanks to the addition of bright cilantro. Smoky bacon and two cheeses add additional, and irresistible, richness.

½ of a 17.3-ounce package frozen puff pastry (I sheet), thawed for 30 minutes

8 strips bacon

2 4-ounce cans diced green chiles, drained

I cup shredded Monterey Jack cheese

I cup shredded sharp Cheddar cheese

1¼ cups half and half

¼ cup chopped fresh cilantro leaves

4 large eggs

½ teaspoon salt

* Preheat oven to 400°F. Roll out puff pastry on a lightly floured surface to an 11-inch square. Transfer to 9-inch diameter glass pie plate. Trim edges. Place in refrigerator.

* Cook bacon in a large heavy skillet over medium-high heat until brown and crisp. Transfer to paper-towel-lined plate to drain. Crumble bacon.

* Sprinkle bacon, chiles, and cheeses over prepared crust. In a medium bowl beat half and half, cilantro, eggs, and salt to blend. Pour half and half mixture into crust.

* Bake quiche until knife inserted into center comes out clean, about 35–40 minutes. Let quiche stand 5 minutes. Cut quiche into wedges and serve. Makes 6 servings.

Sausage & Tomato Quiche

On a busy weekday night, a simple yet satisfying dinner recipe is better than money in the bank. This hearty quiche fits the bill.

½	of a 17.3-ounce package frozen puff pastry (1 sheet), thawed for 30 minutes
½	pound bulk Italian sausage
1	cup shredded mozzarella cheese
2	large egg yolks
1	large egg
1	teaspoon dried oregano, crumbled
½	teaspoon salt
⅛	teaspoon dried red pepper flakes
2	cups whipping cream
1	large tomato, halved crosswise, seeded, and thinly sliced

✳ Preheat oven to 400°F. Roll out puff pastry on a lightly floured surface to an 11-inch square. Transfer to 9-inch diameter glass pie plate. Trim edges. Place in refrigerator.

✳ In a large nonstick pan set over medium-high heat cook the sausage until no longer pink, breaking up with the back of a spoon. Cool.

✳ Place cheese and sausage in prepared crust. In a medium bowl beat together yolks, egg, oregano, salt, and red pepper flakes. Whisk in cream. Pour over cheese and sausage. Place tomato in circular pattern atop quiche.

✳ Bake until tester inserted in center comes out clean, about 35–40 minutes. Let stand 10 minutes. Serve warm. Makes 6 servings.

✳ *Pot Pies, Pizza, Quiche & Other Entrées*

Greek Spinach Quiche

Eating your spinach suddenly got very easy. A light crust made from puff pastry reveals a satisfying combination of healthful spinach with the unmistakable goodness of fresh eggs and Greek herbs.

½ of a 17.3-ounce package frozen puff pastry (1 sheet), thawed for 30 minutes

1 3-ounce package cream cheese, room temperature

⅓ cup half and half

3 large eggs

1 10-ounce package frozen chopped spinach, thawed, squeezed of excess liquid

¾ cup crumbled feta cheese

2 green onions, sliced

2 teaspoons dried dill

¼ teaspoon salt

¼ teaspoon pepper

✳ Preheat oven to 400°F. Roll out puff pastry on a lightly floured surface to an 11-inch square. Transfer to 9-inch diameter glass pie plate. Trim edges. Place in refrigerator.

✳ In medium bowl beat cream cheese with electric mixer until smooth. Gradually beat in half and half and eggs. With a wooden spoon, mix in the spinach, feta, green onions, dill, salt, and pepper. Pour mixture into prepared crust.

✳ Bake until crust is golden brown and filling is set, about 35–40 minutes. Cool 10 minutes before serving. Makes 6 servings.

Normandy Potato Tart

Crisp-tender potato slices plus crème fraîche plus puff pastry equals a guaranteed crowd pleaser.

½	of a 17.3-ounce package frozen puff pastry (I sheet), thawed for 30 minutes
2	tablespoons extra-virgin olive oil, divided
⅔	cup crème fraîche (or sour cream)
2	cloves garlic, thinly sliced
3	medium, waxy potatoes (about 14 ounces), peeled, cooked, and thinly sliced into rounds
I	teaspoon dried thyme leaves
	Salt and freshly ground black pepper

✳ Line a baking sheet with parchment paper. On a lightly floured surface unfold pastry sheet and gently roll out to a 14x12-inch rectangle. Transfer pastry to baking sheet and prick all over with a fork. Chill pastry, covered, at least 30 minutes and up to I day.

✳ Preheat oven to 400°F.

✳ Brush the pastry with I tablespoon of the olive oil. Spread with crème fraîche and sprinkle with the garlic slices. Cover with the potato slices and drizzle with remaining olive oil. Sprinkle with thyme leaves and generously season with salt and pepper.

✳ Bake in the center of the oven until the pastry is golden at the edges and the cream is bubbling gently, about 30–35 minutes. Remove, let sit for 5 minutes, then cut and serve. Makes 4 servings.

Pot Pies, Pizza, Quiche & Other Entrées

Roasted Tomato Tart with Fresh Herbs

If there is anything better than summer tomatoes, I don't know about it. Here they are roasted to concentrate their flavor and sweetness, then combined with fresh herbs for an exquisite vegetarian tart.

12	large garlic cloves, peeled
1	teaspoon plus 2 tablespoons olive oil, divided use
4	red plum tomatoes, halved lengthwise
4	yellow tomatoes, halved lengthwise
¼	teaspoon salt
½	teaspoon ground black pepper
½	of a 17.3-ounce package frozen puff pastry (1 sheet), thawed for 30 minutes
1¼	cups grated Gruyère cheese, divided use
2	teaspoons chopped fresh thyme
2	teaspoons chopped fresh rosemary

✳ Preheat oven to 375°F.

✳ Place garlic on 6-inch square of foil; drizzle garlic with 1 teaspoon oil. Seal foil packet. Toss tomatoes, salt, pepper, and 2 tablespoons oil in bowl. Arrange tomatoes, cut side up, on rimmed baking sheet. Drizzle any juices in bowl over tomatoes.

✳ Place garlic packet on same sheet. Bake tomatoes and garlic packet until garlic is soft, about 50 minutes. Remove from oven; increase temperature to 400°F.

✳ Meanwhile, line a baking sheet with parchment paper. Roll out puff pastry on a lightly floured surface to 10-inch square; transfer to prepared sheet. Using fork, pierce pastry all over. Chill 20 minutes.

✳ Sprinkle ¾ cup cheese over pastry, leaving 1-inch plain border. Arrange tomatoes in alternating colors, cut side up, over cheese in 4 rows. Place garlic cloves between tomatoes. Sprinkle with thyme, rosemary, and remaining ½ cup cheese. Bake tart until golden, about 25 minutes. Serve warm or at room temperature. Makes 4 servings.

Smoked Salmon & Leek Tart

I prefer Nova salmon for this sophisticated yet understated French tart because it is milder and less salty than other smoked salmon. Both the puff pastry crust and leek filling can be prepared up to one day ahead. The puff pastry can be covered with plastic wrap and stored at room temperature, and the leek filling can be covered and refrigerated until ready to use.

½   of a 17.3-ounce package frozen puff pastry (1 sheet), thawed for 30 minutes

1   tablespoon olive oil

2   small leeks (white and pale green parts only), halved, thinly sliced crosswise

1   cup heavy whipping cream

2   4-ounce packages herbed soft fresh goat cheese, room temperature

4   ounces (half of an 8-ounce package) cream cheese, room temperature

1   tablespoon fresh lemon juice

2   teaspoons chopped fresh thyme

    Salt and pepper, to taste

2   large eggs

4   ounces thinly sliced smoked salmon

2   tablespoons plain dried breadcrumbs

✳ Preheat oven to 350°F. Roll out puff pastry on lightly floured surface to a 12-inch square.

✳ Line a 9-inch-diameter tart pan with removable bottom with pastry, cutting off excess at edge. Using fork, pierce dough all over. Freeze pastry 5 minutes. Cover pastry with aluminum foil. Fill with dried beans or pie weights. Bake pastry 15 minutes. Remove weights and foil. Bake crust until golden, about 5 minutes longer. Cool completely on rack.

✳ Preheat oven to 425°F. Heat olive oil in a large heavy skillet over medium heat. Add sliced leeks and sauté until soft, about 5 minutes. Add whipping cream and simmer 5 minutes. Let mixture cool.

✳ In a large bowl using wooden spoon beat goat cheese and cream cheese until well blended. Stir in leek mixture, lemon juice, and thyme. Season mixture to taste with salt and pepper. Stir in eggs 1 at a time, blending well after each addition.

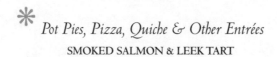

Pot Pies, Pizza, Quiche & Other Entrées

Spread half of filling over bottom of crust. Top with smoked salmon. Top salmon with remaining filling. Sprinkle with breadcrumbs.

 Bake tart until filling is set, about 30 minutes. Transfer to platter. Let tart cool to room temperature. Cut tart into wedges and serve. Makes 6 servings.

Straightforward and slightly unusual, this galette—essentially a French tart—is a very appealing combination of flavors.

½	of a 17.3-ounce package frozen puff pastry (1 sheet), thawed for 30 minutes
¼	cup olive oil
1	4-ounce package goat cheese, room temperature
4	slices thick-cut bacon, cooked crisp, cooled, and coarsely chopped
½	teaspoon chopped fresh thyme leaves
¼	teaspoon freshly ground black pepper
½	of a medium red onion, thinly sliced
1	cup whole, pitted dates, sliced in half lengthwise
3	tablespoons fresh sliced basil leaves
2–3	teaspoons balsamic vinegar

✳ Preheat the oven to 400°F.

✳ On a lightly floured surface roll out pastry to a 13-inch square. Cut out a 12-inch round and place on a baking sheet lined with parchment paper. Place in the freezer for 15 minutes.

✳ In a small bowl combine the olive oil, goat cheese, bacon, thyme, and pepper and mix until smooth.

✳ Remove the crust from the freezer and spread the bottom with the goat cheese mixture, leaving a 1-inch border. Arrange the red onion slices in a concentric pattern over the tart. Fold the border over the edge of the onions. Bake until the crust is golden and puffed, about 25 minutes. Remove from the oven and transfer to a platter.

✳ Top with the dates and fresh basil and drizzle with balsamic vinegar. Cut into wedges and serve. Makes 4–6 servings.

Gorgonzola & Caramelized Pear Tart with Spring Greens

The robust flavor of Gorgonzola, complemented by sweet pears and a spicy mix of spring greens, makes this a great choice for a light summer supper.

2	tablespoons unsalted butter
4	Bosc pears, peeled, cored, and coarsely chopped
$\frac{1}{4}$	cup dry white wine
1	tablespoon chopped fresh thyme
$\frac{1}{2}$	teaspoon salt
$\frac{1}{4}$	teaspoon ground black pepper
$\frac{1}{3}$	cup chopped toasted walnuts
4	ounces prosciutto, chopped
1	17.3-ounce package frozen puff pastry (2 sheets), thawed for 30 minutes
1	large egg, beaten
4	ounces Gorgonzola or other blue cheese, crumbled
3	cups mesclun greens
2	tablespoons extra virgin olive oil
	Salt and pepper, to taste

✳ Preheat oven to 400°F. Line a large baking sheet with parchment paper and set aside.

✳ In a large heavy skillet melt the butter over medium-high heat. Add the pears and sauté until caramelized, 10–12 minutes, stirring occasionally. Add the wine and cook until dry, about 2 minutes. Add the thyme, salt, and pepper, stir well, and remove from the heat. Add the walnuts and prosciutto and stir well to combine. Let cool.

✳ On a lightly floured surface roll out 1 of the pastry sheets to a 12-inch square. Cut into an 11-inch round. Repeat with second pastry sheet.

✳ Place 1 round on the prepared sheet. Brush a $\frac{1}{2}$-inch border of beaten egg around the outside of the round. Spread the pear mixture evenly across the round. Top with blue cheese. Top with the remaining pastry round. Press down on the edges of the pastry to close, and crimp with a fork to seal. Paint the top pastry with egg and cut small slits in the center to vent.

✳ Bake until golden and puffed, 20–25 minutes.

✳ Remove from the oven and cut into 4 wedges. In a medium bowl toss the mesclun with the olive oil; season with salt and pepper. Divide the mesclun and tart among 4 plates and serve. Makes 4 servings.

Pot Pies, Pizza, Quiche & Other Entrées

Summer Zucchini Tart

Light, yet wholly satisfying, this vegetarian tart begins and ends with the best squash of the season. It will make you hope for an abundance of zucchini in your garden this year.

2	tablespoons olive oil
1	medium onion
2	garlic cloves, minced
2	medium zucchini, quartered lengthwise and thinly sliced
1	14.5-ounce can diced tomatoes, well drained
½	of a 17.3-ounce package frozen puff pastry (1 sheet), thawed for 30 minutes
3	large eggs
1	cup grated Havarti cheese
½	teaspoon salt
¼	teaspoon freshly cracked pepper

✳ Heat the oil in a large skillet over medium heat. Add the onion and garlic, and cook 5 minutes, or until the onion is softened. Stir in the zucchini and sauté just until it begins to soften, about 5 minutes. Mix in the drained tomatoes and raise the heat to medium-high. Cook, stirring often, until the zucchini is tender but not mushy and the juices have evaporated. Cool to room temperature.

✳ Spray a 9-inch tart pan with a removable rim or a glass pie plate with nonstick cooking spray. On a lightly floured surface roll out the puff pastry to an 11-inch square. Fit it into the tart pan or pie plate. Trim off the overhanging pastry. Refrigerate the crust, uncovered, for 15 minutes, or up to 8 hours, covered.

✳ Preheat the oven to 425°F.

✳ Beat the eggs in a large bowl. Stir in the cheese, salt, pepper, and cooled vegetables. Spoon the mixture into the tart pan. Bake 25–30 minutes or until the pastry is deep golden brown and a knife inserted in the center of the tart comes out clean. Remove the outer rim of the tart pan. Let cool on a wire rack for 20 minutes before slicing. Makes 4 servings.

Asparagus–Smoked Gouda Tart

A smoked version of Holland's most famous cheese—Gouda—is the cornerstone of this delectable spring tart. This would also make a terrific appetizer or first course; just slice into eight to ten thin slices rather than four.

½   of a 17.3-ounce package frozen puff pastry (1 sheet), thawed for 30 minutes

2   cups grated smoked Gouda cheese

1½   pounds asparagus (medium thickness)

1   tablespoon olive oil

✳ Preheat oven to 400°F.

✳ On a lightly floured surface roll out the puff pastry to a 16x10-inch rectangle. Trim uneven edges. Place pastry on a baking sheet lined with parchment paper. With a sharp knife, lightly score pastry dough 1 inch in from the edges to mark a rectangle. Using a fork, pierce dough inside the markings at ½-inch intervals. Bake until pale golden, about 10 minutes.

✳ Remove pastry shell from oven and sprinkle with the cheese. Trim the bottoms of the asparagus spears to fit crosswise inside the tart shell; arrange in a single layer over cheese, alternating ends and tips. Brush with olive oil and season with salt and pepper.

✳ Bake until spears are tender, about 20–25 minutes. Makes 4 servings.

✔ **Cook's Note:** *Scoring the dough with a knife ensures that the edges rise evenly; pricking the center of the pastry with a fork keeps it from puffing up too high as it bakes.*

Smoked Salmon–Crème Fraîche Tarts

A quick filling made with crème fraîche, horseradish, chives and a topping of smoked salmon and walnuts creates these boast-worthy tarts. The perfect foil? Just whip up a refreshing salad of mixed mesclun greens dressed with your favorite vinaigrette.

½	of a 17.3-ounce package frozen puff pastry (1 sheet), thawed for 30 minutes
1	large egg, lightly beaten
1	teaspoon water
2	tablespoons snipped fresh chives
3	teaspoons prepared horseradish
1	clove garlic, minced
½	cup purchased crème fraîche (or sour cream)
	Salt and pepper, to taste
3	ounces smoked salmon (lox style), cut into thin strips
3	tablespoons finely chopped red onion
¼	cup chopped walnuts, lightly toasted

✴ Preheat oven to 375°F.

✴ Roll out puff pastry sheet to a 15 x 10-inch rectangle on a lightly floured surface. Cut rectangle in half lengthwise to form two 15 x 5-inch rectangles. From edges of each rectangle, cut 2 lengthwise ¾-inch-wide strips and 2 crosswise ¾-inch-wide strips. Set aside the 8 pastry strips.

✴ Place the pastry rectangles on an ungreased baking sheet. Combine egg and water in a small cup; brush onto the rectangles. Place 4 pastry strips atop edges of each rectangle like a frame, trimming to fit. Brush strips with egg mixture. Prick the pastry rectangles all over with the tines of a fork.

✴ Bake about 18–20 minutes or until light golden brown. Remove from oven. If center portions have puffed higher than edges, prick gently with tines of fork. Cool completely on wire racks.

✴ Stir chives, horseradish, and garlic into crème fraîche; season with salt and pepper to taste. Spread over baked crusts. Arrange salmon on top. Sprinkle with red onion and walnuts. Makes 4 servings.

✔ **Cook's Note:** *Bake the puff pastry as directed up to 24 hours in advance. Cool and loosely cover with foil. Prepare crème fraîche mixture and store tightly covered in the refrigerator. Assemble the tarts just before serving.*

Pot Pies, Pizza, Quiche & Other Entrées

Butternut Squash & Farmer's Cheese Tart

When the weather turns cool, why not take time out for a soul-satisfying dinner with your favorite people? This deeply flavored, autumnal tart will make your duties a simple pleasure.

½   of a 17.3-ounce package frozen puff pastry (I sheet), thawed for 30 minutes

3   tablespoons unsalted butter

12   ounces butternut squash, cut into ½-inch cubes (about 2¾ cups)

3   garlic cloves, minced

¾   teaspoon salt, or more to taste

½   teaspoon freshly ground pepper, or more to taste

⅛   teaspoon ground allspice

4   ounces crumbled farmer's, feta, or goat cheese

I   green onion, chopped

* Line a cookie sheet with parchment paper. On a lightly floured surface roll out the puff pastry to a 10-inch square. Place pastry on cookie sheet and refrigerate for at least 20 minutes.

* Meanwhile, in a large skillet on medium heat melt the butter. Add squash and sauté five minutes. Add garlic, salt, and pepper and sauté until squash is soft, I–2 minutes. Stir in allspice and additional salt and pepper to taste. Cool to room temperature.

* Preheat oven to 400°F.

* Sprinkle three-fourths of the cheese on the pastry, leaving a 1-inch border. Arrange squash mixture on top. Sprinkle with remaining cheese.

* Bake tart for 20–25 minutes or until edge is puffed and golden. Sprinkle with green onion. Serve warm or at room temperature. Makes 4 servings.

Ricotta Tart with Parmesan, Golden Raisins, & Pine Nuts

Light and summery, this impressive entrée belies its short list of ingredients. Pair with a freshly tossed green salad or grilled vegetables for a sublime supper.

1½	cups ricotta cheese
⅓	cup freshly grated Parmesan cheese
3	tablespoons fresh lemon juice
½	teaspoon salt
¼	teaspoon freshly ground pepper
2	tablespoons chopped fresh rosemary
½	of a 17.3-ounce package frozen puff pastry (1 sheet), thawed for 30 minutes
1	small onion, thinly sliced
¾	cup golden raisins
2	tablespoons olive oil, divided use
½	cup pine nuts
¾	cup thinly sliced fresh basil

✳ Preheat oven to 400° F. In a large bowl combine the cheeses, lemon juice, salt, pepper, and rosemary until well blended.

✳ Roll out the pastry on a lightly floured surface to a 9 x 13-inch rectangle. Place on a baking sheet lined with parchment paper. Spread the ricotta mixture on top of the pastry, leaving a ½-inch border around the edges. Fold over the border. Place the onion on top. Sprinkle with raisins and drizzle with 1 tablespoon of the olive oil.

✳ Bake until the pastry is light golden brown, 25–30 minutes. Remove from the oven and drizzle with the remaining olive oil. Meanwhile, in a skillet over low heat toast the pine nuts until fragrant and golden, about 5 minutes. Sprinkle with the nuts and fresh basil. Serve warm. Makes 4 servings.

Leek and Gruyère Tart

Lightly sautéing the leeks is the only step for this tart that takes a bit of time. The result is wonderful; the pungent, light lemon aroma of the thyme melds perfectly with the tender leeks and nutty Gruyère.

½ of a 17.3-ounce package frozen puff pastry (1 sheet), thawed for 30 minutes

2 tablespoons extra-virgin olive oil

3 medium leeks, white and tender green, halved lengthwise, thinly sliced cross-wise and rinsed well

1½ teaspoons dried thyme
Salt and pepper, to taste

2 cups grated Gruyère cheese

3 ounces thinly sliced prosciutto

* On a lightly floured surface roll out the pastry to a 13-inch square. Fold the corners in and lightly roll the pastry into a rough round. Transfer to a baking sheet lined with parchment paper. Refrigerate 20 minutes.

* In a large skillet heat the olive oil over medium-high heat. Add the leeks and thyme and season with salt and pepper and cook over moderate heat, stirring occasionally, until softened, about 5 minutes. Cool to room temperature.

* Preheat the oven to 475°F.

* Sprinkle half of the cheese over the pastry, leaving a 1-inch border. Spread the leeks over the cheese. Cover with the prosciutto; sprinkle on the remaining cheese. Season with salt and pepper. Fold up the tart edge to form a rim.

* Bake tart for 20–22 minutes, until golden and bubbling. Blot any excess fat with a paper towel. Cut the tart into wedges. Makes 4 servings.

Fresh Fig and Gorgonzola Tart

It may sound like an unlikely partnership for a tart, but lush, fresh figs together with salty-sweet Gorgonzola is just about the most satisfying combination around.

½ of a 17.3-ounce package frozen puff pastry (1 sheet), thawed for 30 minutes

1 cup crumbled Gorgonzola or other blue cheese

1 tablespoon chopped fresh rosemary

4 fresh black Mission figs, each cut crosswise into 6 slices

✳ Preheat the oven to 350°F. Line a baking sheet with parchment paper.

✳ On a lightly floured surface roll out the pastry to a 10-inch square. Place pastry on the prepared sheet; freeze for 5 minutes.

✳ Using a fork, prick the dough all over. Cover the pastry with a sheet of parchment and another baking sheet.

✳ Bake for about 18–20 minutes or until the pastry is golden and crisp. Remove the baking sheet and the top layer of parchment. Scatter the cheese and rosemary over the pastry and arrange the figs on top.

✳ Bake for 5 minutes, until the cheese is melted and the figs are warm. Makes 4 servings.

Pot Pies, Pizza, Quiche & Other Entrées

Fontina, Polenta & Sage Tart

Multiple textures and flavors—fragrant sage, smooth polenta, and creamy, nutty cheese—combine in this unusual and substantial vegetarian tart.

½   of a 17.3-ounce package frozen puff pastry (1 sheet), thawed for 30 minutes

1   large egg, lightly beaten

2   tablespoons unsalted butter

2   medium onions, thinly sliced

2   cups milk

⅓   cup instant polenta
     Salt and freshly ground pepper

1   cup grated Fontina cheese (about 4 ounces)

2   teaspoons finely chopped sage, plus whole leaves for garnish

✳ Preheat the oven to 475° F. Line a baking sheet with parchment paper.

✳ On a lightly floured surface roll out the pastry to a 12-inch square. Trim the edges to form a neat square. Cut a ½-inch-wide strip from each of the 4 sides of the pastry. Brush the pastry square lightly with the beaten egg, then arrange the strips along the edges to form a raised border. Using a fork, prick the bottom of the crust all over.

✳ Bake 15–18 minutes, or until it is golden and the border has risen; use a fork to flatten any bubbles.

✳ Meanwhile, in a large skillet over medium-high heat melt the butter. Add the onions; cover and cook, stirring frequently, until softened and browned, about 10 minutes. Remove from the heat.

✳ In a medium saucepan bring the milk to a boil. Add the polenta and whisk until smooth. Cook over moderate heat, stirring, until thickened, about 5 minutes. Season with salt and pepper and stir in the onions, Fontina, and chopped sage. Spread the polenta in the crust.

✳ Bake the tart 5–7 minutes, or until the top is lightly browned. Garnish with sage leaves and serve. Makes 4 servings.

Pot Pies, Pizza, Quiche & Other Entrées ✳

Thai Shrimp Turnovers

Shrimp, lime, coconut milk, and vegetables mingle in a complex-tasting curry, easily achieved with supermarket-ready ingredients. Envelopes of puff pastry add plenty of style.

3	tablespoons butter
½	pound button mushrooms, sliced
⅓	cup finely chopped onion
1	cup canned unsweetened coconut milk
½	cup dry white wine
½	cup canned low-salt chicken broth
1	tablespoon mild curry powder
1	teaspoon fresh lime juice
1	teaspoon grated lime zest
1	10-ounce package frozen chopped spinach, thawed, squeezed dry
¼	cup chopped fresh cilantro leaves
	Salt and pepper, to taste
1	17.3-ounce package frozen puff pastry (2 sheets), thawed for 30 minutes
32	uncooked medium-large shrimp, peeled, deveined

✳ In a large heavy skillet melt the butter over medium-high heat. Add mushrooms and onion; sauté 5 minutes. Add coconut milk, wine, and broth. Boil until mixture is reduced to 1 cup, about 12 minutes. Mix in curry powder, lime juice and lime zest, spinach, and cilantro. Season with salt and pepper to taste. Cool to room temperature.

✳ Preheat oven to 375°F.

✳ Roll out 1 pastry sheet on lightly floured surface to a 12-inch square. With one point of square facing you, place half of spinach mixture on bottom half of 1 square. Top spinach mixture with half of the shrimp. Brush pastry edges with water. Fold unfilled half of pastry over filling, forming triangle. Press edges of pastry closed with tines of fork. Place pastry on large baking sheet lined with parchment paper. Repeat with remaining pastry, spinach mixture, and shrimp.

✳ Bake pastries 20–22 minutes or until puffed and golden brown. Serve warm. Makes 2 large turnovers, serving 4.

✔ **Cook's Note:** *The filling can prepared up to 1 day in advance. Cover and refrigerate until ready to use.*

✳ *Pot Pies, Pizza, Quiche & Other Entrées*

Spanikopita Pockets

Spanikopita is a savory Greek spinach pie made with spinach, cheese, eggs, and layers of phyllo dough. This version of the traditional pastry is wonderfully light, and the spinach-feta filling is infused with the bright flavors of garlic, herbs, and lemon.

I	10-ounce package frozen chopped spinach, thawed, squeezed dry
4	green onions, chopped
I½	cups crumbled feta cheese
I	cup shredded mozzarella cheese
2	garlic cloves, minced
I	tablespoon dried dill
¼	teaspoon ground nutmeg
	Juice and grated zest of I medium lemon
	Salt and pepper, to taste
I	17.3-ounce package frozen puff pastry (2 sheets), thawed for 30 minutes
I	large egg, lightly beaten

✴ Preheat oven to 400°F.

✴ In a large bowl mix the spinach, onions, cheeses, garlic, dill, nutmeg, lemon juice, and lemon zest until blended. Season with salt and pepper to taste. Set aside.

✴ On a lightly floured surface roll out each puff pastry sheet to a 12-inch square. Cut each square into four 6-inch squares. Top each 6-inch square with ¼ cup of the spinach mixture. Moisten pastry edges lightly with water. Fold each pastry square over filling to form triangle; seal edges with fork. Brush tops of turnovers with egg. Make 2 or 3 slits in top of each turnover with sharp knife. Place on baking sheets lined with parchment paper.

✴ Bake 18–20 minutes or until golden brown. Serve warm or at room temperature. Makes 8 servings.

Mini Beef Wellingtons with Mushrooms & Gorgonzola

This sumptuous version of beef Wellington, enriched with salty-sweet Gorgonzola and sautéed mushrooms, is a welcome change of pace.

8   6-ounce center-cut filets mignons (about 1½-inches thick)
    Salt and pepper, to taste
2   tablespoons vegetable oil
8   large mushrooms (about ½ pound total)
2   tablespoons unsalted butter
2   tablespoons finely chopped shallot
4   cloves garlic, minced
2   large eggs, lightly beaten
1   17.3-ounce package frozen puff pastry (2 sheets), thawed for 30 minutes
½   cup crumbled Gorgonzola

✳ Pat filets mignons dry and season with salt and pepper. Heat oil in a large skillet over medium-high heat. Sear filets mignons on both sides. Remove filets to a plate. Loosely cover filets with plastic wrap and chill until cold, about 1 hour.

✳ Thinly slice mushrooms, and in a heavy skillet cook in butter with shallot, garlic, and salt and pepper to taste over moderate heat, stirring, until mushrooms are lightly browned. Transfer mushroom mixture to a bowl to cool completely. In a small bowl lightly beat eggs with a fork to make an egg wash.

✳ On a lightly floured surface roll out puff pastry sheets into two 14-inch squares. Trim edges to form two 13-inch squares. Cut each square into 4 squares.

✳ Put 1 tablespoon Gorgonzola in center of 1 square and top with one-eighth of the mushroom mixture. Top mushroom mixture with a filet mignon, pressing it down gently, and wrap 2 opposite corners of puff pastry over filet, overlapping them. Seal seam with egg wash. Wrap remaining 2 corners of pastry over filet and seal in same manner. Seal any gaps with egg wash and press pastry around filet to enclose completely.

✳ Arrange beef Wellington, seam-side down, on a baking pan lined with parchment paper. Make 7 more beef Wellingtons in same manner. Chill remaining egg wash for brushing on pastry just before baking. Chill beef Wellingtons, loosely covered, at least 1 hour and up to 1 day.

* Preheat oven to 425°F.

* Brush top and sides of each beef Wellington with some remaining egg wash and bake 20–30 minutes, or until pastry is golden and the meat temperature is 117°F. Serve immediately. Makes 8 servings.

Chicken & Boursin Bundles

You would never guess that such a sensational main course was so easy to prepare. The Boursin—a buttery-smooth, herbed cheese—melts into a sublime sauce inside each bundle, creating a fine foil to the moist chicken and crisp pastry wrapper.

4	boneless chicken breast halves (about 6 ounces each)
	Salt and pepper, to taste
2	tablespoons butter
1	large egg
1	tablespoon water
½	of a 17.3-ounce package frozen puff pastry (1 sheet), thawed for 30 minutes
1	4-ounce container garlic and herb spreadable cheese (e.g., Boursin® or Alouette®)
¼	cup chopped fresh chives

✳ Sprinkle chicken with salt and pepper. In a large skillet set over medium-high heat, melt the butter. Add chicken and cook until browned on both sides. Remove chicken to a plate. Cover and refrigerate 15 minutes or up to 24 hours.

✳ In a small cup mix egg and water with a fork. Preheat oven to 400°F.

✳ Unfold pastry on lightly floured surface and roll out to a 14-inch square. Cut into 4 squares.

✳ Spread about 2 tablespoons of the cheese spread in center of each square. Sprinkle with 1 tablespoon chives and top with a cooled chicken breast. Brush edges of squares with egg mixture. Fold each corner to center on top of chicken and seal edges. Place seam-side down on ungreased baking sheet. Brush with egg mixture.

✳ Bake the bundles 24–27 minutes or until golden brown. Serve immediately. Makes 4 servings.

Pot Pies, Pizza, Quiche & Other Entrées

CHICKEN & BOURSIN BUNDLES

Salmon Wellington

Puff pastry elevates salmon fillets to sophisticated new heights. And it's very manageable for dinner parties if you assemble the salmon pastries ahead of time. Pop the Wellingtons in the oven while your guests enjoy appetizers—you'll need little more than a simple salad or steamed asparagus to round out the meal.

I	17.3-ounce package frozen puff pastry (2 sheets), thawed for 30 minutes
4	$\frac{3}{4}$-inch-thick 6-ounce skinless salmon fillets
	Salt and pepper, to taste
6	tablespoons minced shallots, divided use
6	teaspoons chopped fresh tarragon, divided use
I	large egg, lightly beaten
$\frac{1}{2}$	cup dry white wine
$\frac{1}{2}$	cup white wine vinegar
$\frac{1}{2}$	cup (I stick) cold butter, diced
	Salt and pepper, to taste

✳ Preheat oven to 425°F.

✳ Roll out each pastry sheet on lightly floured surface to 12-inch square. Cut each in half, forming four 12x6-inch rectangles.

✳ Place I salmon fillet in center of each rectangle, about 3 inches in from and parallel to I short edge. Sprinkle each fillet with salt, pepper, I tablespoon shallots, and I teaspoon tarragon. Brush edges of rectangles with some egg. Fold long sides of pastry over fillets. Fold short edge of pastry over fillets and roll up pastry, enclosing fillets. Seal edges of pastry.

✳ Place pastries, seam-side down, on baking sheet. Brush with beaten egg.

✳ Bake pastries until golden brown, about 18–20 minutes. Remove from oven; let stand 10 minutes. Meanwhile, in small heavy saucepan boil wine, vinegar, and remaining 2 tablespoons shallots until liquid is reduced to 6 tablespoons, about 8 minutes. Remove pan from heat. Add butter I piece at a time, whisking until melted before adding next piece. Whisk in remaining 2 teaspoons tarragon. Season sauce with salt and pepper.

✳ Serve pastries with the sauce alongside. Makes 4 servings.

Pot Pies, Pizza, Quiche & Other Entrées ✳

Pork Wellington

Pork tenderloin is incredibly versatile. Here it takes on upscale flair thanks to the aromatic, piney-lemon flavor of rosemary, fresh spinach, and a puff pastry casing.

1	tablespoon olive oil
1	small onion, chopped
2	cloves garlic, chopped
1	5-ounce bag prewashed baby spinach
2	tablespoons Dijon mustard
	Salt and pepper, to taste
1	teaspoon chopped fresh rosemary
½	teaspoon salt
¼	teaspoon black pepper
1	1-pound pork tenderloin
½	of a 17.3-ounce package frozen puff pastry (1 sheet), thawed for 30 minutes
1	large egg
1	tablespoon water

✳ Preheat the oven to 425°F.

✳ Heat oil in medium-size skillet over medium heat. Add onion and garlic; cook 10 minutes, until softened. Add spinach; cook until spinach is wilted and liquid evaporates, about 3–5 minutes. Remove from heat. Mix in the mustard. Season with salt and pepper to taste. Set aside.

✳ In small bowl mix the rosemary, ½ teaspoon salt, and ¼ teaspoon pepper. Rub over the pork.

✳ Unfold the pastry sheet on a lightly floured work surface. Roll out pastry to a 13-inch square. Spoon onion-spinach mixture into 3-inch-wide mound down center. Place pork on top of spinach mixture, folding over pastry ends if necessary. Wrap pastry over tenderloin to cover, tucking ends under. Make 3 slashes in top of pastry. In a small bowl whisk together the egg and water. Brush pastry with the egg wash. Transfer to a rimmed baking sheet lined with parchment paper.

✳ Roast the pork 35–40 minutes or until instant-read thermometer inserted into tenderloin registers 140°F and pastry is golden brown. If pastry begins to get too brown, cover loosely with aluminum foil. Using 2 large spatulas, transfer roast to a wire rack placed over a dish. Let stand 10 minutes. Slice and serve warm. Makes 6 servings.

✳

Pot Pies, Pizza, Quiche & Other Entrées

Gaucho Beef Roll with Chimichurri

Inspired by Argentinean flavors, this impressive entrée is not only easy to prepare but amazingly flavorful. It really benefits from the bright, fresh flavors of the accompanying chimichurri sauce.

1	pound extra-lean ground beef
1	small onion, grated
2	large eggs
1	teaspoon minced canned chipotle chile in adobo sauce, plus 1 teaspoon adobo sauce
	Salt and pepper, to taste
1	tablespoon vegetable oil
½	cup dry breadcrumbs
¼	cup dry red wine
½	of 17.3-ounce package frozen puff pastry (1 sheet), thawed for 30 minutes
1	cup packed fresh flat leaf parsley
½	cup extra virgin olive oil
¼	cup red wine vinegar
¼	cup packed fresh cilantro
2	garlic cloves, peeled
½	teaspoon ground cumin
¼	teaspoon dried crushed red pepper
½	teaspoon salt

✴ In a large bowl mix the ground beef, onion, eggs, chipotle chile, and adobo sauce. Season with salt and pepper.

✴ Heat oil in a large skillet set over medium heat. Brown beef mixture. Cool 15 minutes. Mix in the breadcrumbs and red wine.

✴ Preheat oven to 425°F. Roll out the puff pastry on a lightly floured surface into a 10-inch square. Place beef mixture along the long edge of the pastry. Roll up and tuck ends under. Place on an ungreased cookie sheet.

✴ Bake 18–20 minutes or until golden.

✴ Meanwhile, prepare chimichurri by placing the parsley, olive oil, vinegar, cilantro, garlic, cumin, red pepper, and salt in a food processor or blender. Process until smooth and transfer to a bowl.

✴ Slice the warm beef roll and serve with the chimichurri. Makes 4–6 servings.

Pot Pies, Pizza, Quiche & Other Entrées ✴

❋ Smoked Salmon and Eggs in Puff Pastry ❋

Elegant enough for a very special brunch, this would also make an extravagant breakfast for a birthday or Christmas morning.

9	large eggs, divided use
½	cup milk
¼	teaspoon salt
¼	teaspoon pepper
1	tablespoon butter
1	4-ounce container garlic and herb spreadable cheese (e.g., Boursin® or Alouette®)
1	teaspoon dried dill
½	of 17.3-ounce package frozen puff pastry (1 sheet), thawed for 30 minutes
3	ounces thinly sliced smoked salmon (lox-style)
⅔	cup grated Swiss cheese
1	tablespoon water

❋ Line a baking sheet with parchment paper.

❋ In medium bowl whisk 8 of the eggs, milk, salt, and pepper. In large skillet melt butter over medium heat; pour in egg mixture. Cook until eggs are just barely set. Remove from heat. Dot with the spreadable cheese and sprinkle with dill. Gently stir until combined. Cool to room temperature.

❋ Preheat oven to 375°F.

❋ Unfold pastry on a lightly floured surface and roll out to a 17 x 12-inch rectangle. Place on prepared baking sheet (short sides may extend over sides of sheet). Arrange the smoked salmon crosswise down the center one-third of pastry to within 1 inch of top and bottom edges. Spoon scrambled eggs over salmon. Sprinkle with Swiss cheese. Whisk the water and remaining egg in a small cup. Brush edges of pastry with egg mixture.

❋ Fold a short side of pastry over filling. Fold remaining short side over top; seal. Seal ends well and brush top of pastry with egg mixture.

❋ Bake 22–25 minutes or until pastry is golden brown and filling is heated through. Makes 6 servings.

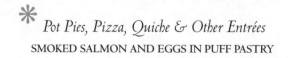

Pot Pies, Pizza, Quiche & Other Entrées

SMOKED SALMON AND EGGS IN PUFF PASTRY

Puff Pastry Po'Boys

There are many ways to make these iconic New Orleans sandwiches, but doing it with puff pastry in place of bread makes for an exceptional new twist.

1	17.3-ounce package frozen puff pastry (2 sheets), thawed for 30 minutes
1½	cups shredded Mozzarella cheese
1½	cups shredded Cheddar cheese
6	ounces thinly sliced ham
6	ounces thinly sliced roast beef
4	ounces pepperoni
½	cup jarred marinara sauce
2	large eggs
2	tablespoons water

✳ Preheat the oven to 350°F. Line a baking sheet with parchment paper.

✳ On a lightly floured surface roll out puff pastry sheets to two 14-inch squares. Cut each square into 4 squares.

✳ Lay 4 of the pastry squares on a flat surface and layer with the cheeses, meats, and a generous spoonful of the marinara sauce. Place another square of puff pastry on top of the filling. Using hands, lightly press the pastry around the filling. Using a fork, press the ends of the pastry together.

✳ Whisk the eggs and water together in a small bowl. Place the pockets on prepared baking sheet. Using a pastry brush, lightly brush each pocket with egg mixture.

✳ Bake until golden brown, about 12–15 minutes. Serve warm. Makes 8 servings.

Cream of Portobello Soup with Puff Pastry Tops

Silky-smooth with crisp-tender tops, this seductive soup packs a punch of earthy flavors.

1½ pounds portobello mushrooms, stemmed

2 tablespoons unsalted butter

2 onions, chopped

Salt and pepper, to taste

3 cups canned, low-sodium chicken broth

1 cup heavy cream

3 tablespoons medium-dry sherry

¼ cup thinly sliced fresh chives

1 17.3-ounce package frozen puff pastry (2 sheets), thawed for 30 minutes

1 large egg, lightly beaten

✳ Quarter and thinly slice the mushrooms. Heat the butter in a heavy saucepan over medium-high heat. Add the onions and mushrooms, season with salt and pepper, and cook, stirring occasionally, until softened and any liquid the mushrooms give off has evaporated. Add broth and cream and simmer 15 minutes.

✳ Using a handheld blender, purée the soup. Stir in sherry and season with salt and pepper. Cool to lukewarm.

✳ Divide the soup among 4 deep (about 2 cups), oven-safe bowls about 5 inches in diameter, and stir some of the chives into each.

✳ On a lightly floured surface roll out puff pastry sheets into two 14-inch squares. Cut each square into two 6½-inch-diameter circles.

✳ Brush the inner edges of the pastry disks with some of the beaten egg. Invert the pastry discs (egg washed-side down) over the soup bowls and press the edges onto the sides to seal. Brush the tops with some of the beaten egg. Refrigerate 1 hour.

✳ Preheat the oven to 400°F. Put the soup bowls on a baking sheet and bake until pastry is golden brown and puffed, about 25–28 minutes. Makes 4 servings.

Sausage, Cranberries & Stuffing Pastry

The secret to leisurely eating? Soul-satisfying suppers such as this sausage-cranberry pastry. It packs a main dish and a side dish in one streamlined recipe, making both mealtime and meal preparation sheer pleasure.

I	tablespoon water
2	large eggs, divided use
½	pound bulk pork sausage
I	cup seasoned dry stuffing
4	green onions, chopped
I	cup chopped mushrooms
½	cup dried cranberries
½	teaspoon dry rubbed sage
½	of a 17.3-ounce package frozen puff pastry (I sheet), thawed for 30 minutes
	Jarred or homemade gravy, warmed (optional)

✳ Preheat oven to 375°F. In a small bowl beat the water and I of the eggs with a fork. Set aside.

✳ In a medium bowl mix the sausage, stuffing, remaining egg, green onions, mushrooms, cranberries, and sage until thoroughly blended.

✳ Unfold pastry sheet on lightly floured surface. Cut slits I-inch apart from outer edge up to fold mark on each side of pastry. Spoon sausage mixture down center of pastry. Starting at one end, fold pastry strips over sausage mixture, alternating sides, to cover sausage mixture. Place on baking sheet. Brush with egg mixture.

✳ Bake 30–35 minutes or until golden. Slice and serve warm with gravy, if desired. Makes 4 servings.

Ham & Cheese Florentine

Surprisingly elegant, this entrée is a snap to prepare with simple ingredients from the grocery store.

- 1 large egg
- 1 tablespoon water
- 2 green onions, chopped
- ½ teaspoon dried oregano leaves
- ½ of a 17.3-ounce package frozen puff pastry (1 sheet), thawed for 30 minutes
- 1 pound sliced deli ham
- 1 cup baby spinach leaves
- 4 ounces sliced Swiss cheese

✱ Preheat oven to 400°F. In a small bowl beat the egg and water with a fork. In a separate small bowl mix the onions and oregano.

✱ Unfold pastry on lightly floured surface. Roll out to a 16x12-inch rectangle. With short side facing you, layer ham, spinach, and cheese on bottom half of pastry to within 1-inch of edges. Sprinkle with onion mixture.

✱ Starting at short side, roll up like a jelly roll. Place seam-side down on baking sheet. Tuck ends under to seal. Brush with egg mixture.

✱ Bake 22–25 minutes or until golden. Slice and serve warm. Makes 4 servings.

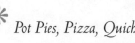

Pot Pies, Pizza, Quiche & Other Entrées

Cookies & Other Petite Confections

Bowtie Cookies

These whimsical almond cookies are perfect for entertaining. The contrast between the light, crisp quality of the puff pastry and rich, nutty filling will keep guests coming back for more.

½   of a 17.3-ounce package frozen puff pastry (1 sheet), thawed for 30 minutes
½   cup packaged almond paste
1   large egg, separated
½   cup packed brown sugar
2   teaspoons milk
    Sugar, for sprinkling

＊ Unfold pastry on a lightly floured surface and roll out to a 14-inch square. Cut square in half with a fluted pastry wheel.

＊ Preheat oven to 400°F. Line 2 baking sheets with parchment paper.

＊ In a small mixing bowl crumble the almond paste. Add egg yolk, brown sugar, and milk. Beat with an electric mixer on medium speed until well mixed. Spread filling over 1 pastry half. Place remaining pastry half on top of filling. Using the fluted pastry wheel, cut dough crosswise into 14 1-inch-wide strips.

＊ Cut each strip in half crosswise to make 28 pieces. Twist each piece twice. Place twists about 2 inches apart on prepared sheets. In a small bowl whisk egg white with a fork until frothy; brush over twists. Sprinkle with sugar.

＊ Bake for 12–15 minutes or until golden. Transfer to wire racks to cool. Makes 28 cookies.

✔**Cook's Note:** *The almond filling will be very stiff. To make spreading easier, drop dollops of almond paste mixture uniformly over pastry. Spray a piece of waxed paper with non-stick cooking spray. Press almond paste mixture evenly over entire dough. Spray waxed paper as often as necessary to prevent filling from sticking.*

Chocolate Hazelnut Cookies

Perfect as an everyday treat or as an after-dinner nibble with coffee, these rich and easy cookies will become one of your favorite standbys.

I	17.3-ounce package frozen puff pastry (2 sheets), thawed for 30 minutes
I I	tablespoons chocolate hazelnut spread (e.g., Nutella®)
½	cup chopped hazelnuts (or almonds)
6	teaspoons powdered sugar

✳ Preheat oven to 425°F. Line 2 baking sheets with parchment paper.

✳ On a lightly floured surface roll out the pastry into a 9 x 20–inch rectangle (dough will be very thin). Spread the chocolate hazelnut spread over the pastry, then scatter hazelnuts over the top.

✳ Roll the long sides of the pastry rectangle toward the center; where they meet in the center, dampen with water to secure. Using a sharp knife, cut into about ½-inch slices; place on the baking sheet, and sprinkle with powdered sugar. Place cookies on prepared sheets.

✳ Bake cookies 10–12 minutes until golden brown. Transfer to wire rack and cool completely. Makes 34 cookies.

✳ *Cookies & Other Petite Confections*

Lemon Cream Strudel Sticks

Lemon is an exquisite flavor on its own, but when it's paired with the unexpected flavor of cardamom, it hits an even higher note.

2	3-ounce packages cream cheese, softened
⅓	cup plus 1 tablespoon sugar, divided use
2	teaspoons grated lemon zest
½	teaspoon ground cardamom
1	17.3-ounce package frozen puff pastry (2 sheets), thawed for 30 minutes
3	tablespoons chopped, sliced almonds

✳ Preheat oven to 350°F.

✳ In a small bowl mix the cream cheese, ⅓ cup sugar, lemon zest, and cardamom with an electric mixer set on medium-high speed until blended and smooth; set aside.

✳ Unfold puff pastry sheets on a lightly floured surface. Cut each sheet into six (6) 5 x 3-inch rectangles.

✳ Spread about 1 tablespoon cheese filling over each rectangle to ½-inch from edges. Roll up jelly roll–style, starting from one long side. Moisten edge of dough and pinch edges to seal. Place pastry sticks, seam-sides down, on a lightly greased baking sheet. Make 3–4 diagonal cuts in top of each pastry. Lightly brush with water. Sprinkle with almonds and remaining tablespoon sugar.

✳ Bake 30–35 minutes or until golden brown. Serve warm or cool. Makes 12 strudel sticks.

✔ **Cook's Note:** *Strudel sticks may be made ahead of time. Cool completely and place in freezer containers or bags. To reheat for serving, wrap in foil and heat in a 325°F oven for 15–20 minutes or until heated through.*

Cookies & Other Petite Confections ✳

Spiced Cranberry Pinwheel Cookies

Tart cranberries combine with a symphony of spices in these pretty cookies. A bit of orange adds a lovely background flavor.

½	cup sugar
2	teaspoons ground cinnamon
2	teaspoons grated orange zest
½	teaspoon ground allspice
½	teaspoon ground ginger
¼	teaspoon ground nutmeg
	Additional sugar
I	17.3-ounce package frozen puff pastry (2 sheets), thawed for 30 minutes
¼	cup (½ stick) unsalted butter, melted
2	cups chopped dried cranberries, divided use
I	large egg, lightly beaten

✳ In small bowl mix the sugar, cinnamon, orange zest, allspice, ginger, and nutmeg.

✳ Sprinkle work surface generously with additional sugar; place I puff pastry sheet on sugared surface. Cut sheet in half, forming two 9 x 4½-inch rectangles. Brush each rectangle generously with some of melted butter, leaving I-inch plain border along I long side of each. Sprinkle buttered part of each rectangle with I½ tablespoons spiced sugar. Scatter ½ cup cranberries over spiced sugar on each.

✳ Brush border of each with beaten egg. Starting at long side opposite glazed border, tightly roll up each rectangle, pressing firmly to seal long edges. Wrap each log separately in plastic. Repeat with remaining pastry sheet, butter, spiced sugar, cranberries, and egg to create 2 more logs. Chill logs until firm, at least 3 hours and up to I day.

✳ Preheat oven to 400°F. Line a baking sheet with parchment paper.

✳ Using serrated knife, cut 2 logs into ½-inch-thick rounds (keep remaining 2 logs chilled). Arrange rounds on prepared sheets, spacing I inch apart.

✳ Bake cookies 18–20 minutes until golden brown. Cool cookies on sheets on racks 5 minutes. Transfer cookies to racks, bottom side up. Cool completely. Repeat slicing and baking with remaining 2 logs. Makes about 5 dozen cookies.

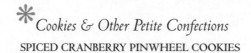

Cookies & Other Petite Confections

Southern Pecan Crisps

For a uniquely sassy, Southern sweet, give these easy, five-ingredient cookies a try.

½   cup packed dark brown sugar

2   tablespoons butter, melted

⅓   cup finely chopped pecans

½   of a 17.3-ounce package frozen puff pastry (1 sheet), thawed for 30 minutes

2   tablespoons powdered sugar

✳ Preheat oven to 400°F. Mix brown sugar, butter, and pecans in a small bowl.

✳ Unfold pastry on lightly floured surface. Roll into 15 x 12-inch rectangle. Cut into twenty (20) 3-inch squares. Press squares into bottoms of 3-inch muffin-pan cups.

✳ Place 1 heaping teaspoon pecan mixture in center of each.

✳ Bake 10–12 minutes or until golden. Remove from pans. Cool on wire rack. Sprinkle with powdered sugar. Makes 20 pastries.

Blueberry-Lemon Twists

These whimsical cookies can do just about anything: bring a smile to a child, cheer up a friend, or make a rainy day a bit brighter. Apricot, raspberry, blackberry, or strawberry jam are equally delicious options in place of the blueberry jam.

¾	cup blueberry jam
½	of a 17.3-ounce package frozen puff pastry (1 sheet), thawed for 30 minutes
½	cup powdered sugar
2	tablespoons heavy cream or milk
1	tablespoon fresh lemon juice

✳ Put oven rack in middle position and preheat oven to 425°F. Line a baking sheet with parchment paper.

✳ In a small saucepan heat the jam over medium-low heat. Stir until just melted; remove from heat.

✳ Roll out pastry on a lightly floured surface to a 12 x 10-inch rectangle, then cut in half lengthwise. Cut each half crosswise into four (4) 5 x 3-inch strips (for a total of 8 strips).

✳ Spread each strip with ½ tablespoon jam, then fold strips in half lengthwise to form 1½-inch-wide strips. Twist each strip 3 times and place on baking sheet. Repeat with remaining pastry and jam.

✳ Bake until golden brown, about 15–18 minutes. Transfer twists to a rack set over a sheet of parchment. Stir together powdered sugar, cream, and lemon juice until smooth, then brush over warm twists. Serve warm. Makes 16 twists.

Pistachio Crisps

I took a lead from a busy friend (and mother of two) who said she loves recipes that have few ingredients but plenty of style. These irresistible, yet refined, cookies fit the bill. All you need is a box of puff pastry dough, some pistachios, and powdered sugar. You can vary the nuts according to what's on hand (or on sale), but the pale green pistachios are especially pretty here.

I   **cup powdered sugar**
I   **cup shelled natural pistachios**
I   **17.3-ounce package frozen puff pastry (2 sheets), thawed for 30 minutes**

✳ Line 2 baking sheets with parchment paper. Blend powdered sugar and nuts in processor until nuts are finely chopped.

✳ Sprinkle 10-inch square area on work surface with ⅓ cup nut sugar; top with pastry sheet. Sprinkle pastry with ⅓ cup nut sugar. Roll out to a 12-inch square. Roll up into 12-inch-long log. Cut into sixteen (16) ¾-inch-wide rounds. Roll out each to 4-inch-diameter round, sprinkling with more nut sugar as needed to prevent sticking. Arrange rounds on prepared sheets. Repeat with remaining pastry and nut sugar. Cover and chill at least 30 minutes.

✳ Preheat oven to 375°F. Bake pistachio rounds uncovered until brown on bottom and golden on top, reversing sheets after 10 minutes, about 16 minutes total. Transfer crisps to racks and cool. Makes 32 crisps.

Cookies & Other Petite Confections ✳

Shortcut Rugalach Cookies

Rugalach cookies are bite-size, crescent-shaped cookies, typically served during Hanukkah. They are often prepared with a rich cream cheese dough and stuffed with any number of fillings, including raisins and nuts, poppy-seed paste, or jam. This simplified version is lighter and crisper but every bit as delicious.

1	cup raisins
⅔	cup walnuts
⅔	cup plus 2 teaspoons sugar, divided use
1¼	teaspoons ground cinnamon, divided use
1	large egg white
2	teaspoons water
1	17.3-ounce package frozen puff pastry (2 sheets), thawed for 30 minutes

✳ In food processor with knife blade attached, blend raisins, walnuts, ⅔ cup sugar, and 1 teaspoon cinnamon until raisins and walnuts are finely chopped.

✳ In small bowl lightly beat egg white with water. In another small bowl mix remaining 2 teaspoons sugar with remaining ¼ teaspoon cinnamon. Set both bowls aside.

✳ Line 2 baking sheets with parchment paper.

✳ On lightly floured surface roll out 1 pastry sheet to a 14x12-inch rectangle. Cut pastry crosswise in half to make two 7x12-inch rectangles.

✳ Divide raisin mixture into fourths. Sprinkle one-fourth of raisin mixture (rounded ½ cup) on 1 rectangle, leaving ¾-inch border along a 12-inch side. Repeat with another one-fourth of raisin mixture on second rectangle. Lightly brush border on each rectangle with some egg-white mixture. Roll each pastry rectangle, jelly roll–fashion, starting from 12-inch side with filling; pinch seam to seal.

✳ Brush rolls with some egg-white mixture, and sprinkle with half of sugar-cinnamon mixture. Cut each roll crosswise into 12 (about 1-inch-thick) pieces. Place pieces, about 1½ inches apart, seam-side down, on a prepared baking sheet. Repeat, using second puff-pastry sheet and remaining filling. Chill, loosely covered, 20 minutes.

✳ Preheat oven to 375°F. Bake cookies 15–17 minutes, until puffed and golden. Transfer cookies to wire rack. Cool completely. Store cookies in tightly covered container. Makes about 4 dozen cookies.

Cookies & Other Petite Confections

SHORTCUT RUGALACH COOKIES

Cream Cheese Chocolate-Chip Pastry Cookies

This is the best of all worlds: a quick, easy, sumptuous little cookie that tastes like a combination of cheesecake, chocolate chip cookies, and a French croissant. And with only four ingredients, who could ask for anything more?

I	17.3-ounce package frozen puff pastry (2 sheets), thawed for 30 minutes
I	8-ounce package cream cheese, softened
3	tablespoons sugar
I¾	cups miniature semisweet chocolate chips

✳ On a lightly floured surface roll out I puff pastry sheet to a 14x10-inch rectangle. In small bowl beat cream cheese and sugar with electric mixer set on medium speed until smooth.

✳ Spread half of cream cheese mixture over puff pastry, leaving I-inch border on one long side. Sprinkle with half of the chips. Roll up starting at long side covered with cream cheese. Seal end by moistening with water. Repeat steps with remaining puff pastry, cream cheese filling, and chips. Loosely cover with plastic wrap and refrigerate for I hour.

✳ Preheat oven to 375° F. Line 2 baking sheets with parchment paper.

✳ Cut rolls crosswise into ¾-inch-thick slices. Place cut-side down on prepared baking sheets.

✳ Bake 20–25 minutes or until golden brown. Cool on baking sheets for 2 minutes; remove to wire racks to cool completely. Makes 3 dozen cookies.

Jam Pinwheels

Need a batch of homemade cookies in a hurry? Here's your elegant solution. Better still, you probably have all of the ingredients on hand. Be sure to limit the jam filling to ½ teaspoon per cookie—too much, and it will bubble over and burn on the cookie sheet.

1	17.3-ounce package frozen puff pastry (2 sheets), thawed for 30 minutes
1	large egg, lightly beaten
½	cup sugar
½	cup jam or preserves of choice (e.g., blueberry, raspberry, or apricot)
2–3	tablespoons powdered sugar

✱ Line 2 baking sheets with parchment paper.

✱ Roll out 1 puff pastry sheet on a lightly floured surface to a 16x13-inch rectangle. Trim edges neatly, forming 15x12-inch rectangle. Cut rectangle into twenty (20) 3-inch squares.

✱ Using small sharp knife, make 1-inch-long diagonal cut in all 4 corners of 1 square, cutting toward center (do not cut through center). Fold every other point of puff pastry toward center of square, pressing to adhere, to form pinwheel. Repeat with remaining puff pastry squares.

✱ Brush pinwheels lightly with beaten egg. Sprinkle each with ½ teaspoon sugar. Place scant ½ teaspoon jam in center of each. Transfer to a prepared baking sheet. Repeat with remaining puff pastry sheet, glaze, sugar, and jam. Refrigerate, loosely covered with plastic wrap, for 20 minutes.

✱ Preheat oven to 400°F. Bake until pinwheels are golden and puffed, about 11–13 minutes. Using metal spatula, transfer cookies to rack and cool.

✱ Sprinkle cookies with powdered sugar, if desired. Makes 40 cookies.

✱ *Cookies & Other Petite Confections*

Cardamom Palmiers

Crisp, delicate, and glistening with golden sugar, these easy cookies require little more than rolling, slicing, and baking. They are an ideal complement to tea.

½   **cup sugar**
1¼ **teaspoons ground cardamom**
1   **17.3-ounce package frozen puff pastry (2 sheets), thawed for 30 minutes**

✳ Line 2 baking sheets with parchment paper.

✳ Mix the sugar and cardamom in a small dish. Sprinkle some of the cardamom sugar on a work surface and cover it with 1 sheet of puff pastry. Then sprinkle more cardamom sugar evenly over pastry sheet and roll it out into a 10-inch square. Roll in two opposite sides of the pastry sheet square so that the sides meet in the center.

✳ Cut pastry crosswise into ½-inch-thick slices. Dip cut sides of each piece in cardamom sugar and arrange, cut-side down, on prepared baking sheet. Repeat with second pastry sheet. Chill, loosely covered with plastic wrap, for 20 minutes.

✳ Preheat oven to 400°F. Bake palmiers in batches in middle of oven until golden on bottom, about 12 minutes. Turn over and bake until golden on bottom, 5–7 minutes more, then transfer to a rack to cool completely. Makes about 32 palmiers.

Cookies & Other Petite Confections ✳

Cinnamon Pecan Twists

I have probably had more requests for this humble cookie than any other, perhaps because it has such consistently good results. It's a bit like the cinnamon toast fingers you had as a kid, but with a "twist" of grown-up flair.

½   cup packed light brown sugar

½   cup pecans halves

½   teaspoon ground cinnamon

1   17.3-ounce package frozen puff pastry (2 sheets), thawed for 30 minutes

1   large egg, beaten

✷ Combine sugar, pecans, and cinnamon in a mini-chopper and process until sandy. Line 2 baking sheets with parchment paper.

✷ Unfold 1 pastry sheet on lightly floured surface and brush with egg. Spread half of sugar mixture over pastry. Cut into eighteen (18) ½-inch-wide strips. Twist strips. Lay on pans, pushing ends down with your thumb. Freeze 10–15 minutes, until firm. Repeat with remaining sheet of pastry, sugar mixture, and egg.

✷ Preheat oven to 400°F.

✷ Bake twists until golden brown, about 16-18 minutes. Transfer to a wire rack and cool completely. Makes 36 twists.

✷ *Cookies & Other Petite Confections*

Double Ginger Sugar Twists

These crispy cookies, crackly with sugar, get a burst of intensity from two types of peppery ginger.

- 6   tablespoons turbinado ("raw") sugar, divided use
- ½   of a 17.3-ounce package frozen puff pastry (1 sheet), thawed for 30 minutes
- 1   large egg, lightly beaten
- 3   tablespoons finely chopped crystallized ginger
- 1   teaspoon ground ginger

✳ Preheat oven to 350°F. Line a baking sheet with parchment paper.

✳ Sprinkle work surface with 3 tablespoons sugar. Set pastry atop sugar and roll out to thickness of ⅛ inch. Brush with egg.

✳ In small bowl combine remaining 3 tablespoons sugar, crystallized ginger, and ground ginger. Sprinkle over pastry. Cut pastry crosswise into 1-inch-wide strips. Pick up each pastry strip, twist several times and place on prepared baking sheet, pressing ends onto sheet.

✳ Bake until golden brown and crisp, about 16–18 minutes. Transfer to a wire rack and cool completely. Makes 12 twists.

Chocolate Bow Ties

Some days it will be all you can do to resist the temptation of these chocolate cookies, which are as easy to make as they are to devour.

1	17.3-ounce package frozen puff pastry (2 sheets), thawed for 30 minutes
2	tablespoons milk
½	cup granulated sugar
3	tablespoons unsweetened cocoa powder
1	large egg, lightly beaten
3	tablespoons powdered sugar

* Unfold 1 pastry sheet on a lightly floured surface. Brush with some of the milk.

* Combine the sugar and cocoa in small bowl. Sprinkle half of the cocoa-sugar over top of pastry. Refold pastry into thirds to original shape. Trim long sides of rectangle to remove rounded edges.

* Lay rolling pin lengthwise on rectangle; roll until 3½ inches wide. Cut across width in ½-inch-wide strips. Give each strip half twist; pinch center. Place on prepared baking sheet, spacing 3 inches apart. Brush with beaten egg.

* Repeat with remaining pastry sheet, cocoa sugar, and egg. Refrigerate, loosely covered with plastic wrap, for 30 minutes.

* Preheat oven to 400°F. Bake bow ties 7–9 minutes until cookies begin to brown on bottom. Turn over; bake 10 minutes longer. Transfer bow ties to cooling rack and cool completely. Sprinkle with powdered sugar. Makes 40 bow ties.

Apricot Swirls

These fragrant treats would be great served with a tall iced tea, a good book, and an afternoon free of errands.

1⅓	cups dried apricots
⅓	cup packed light brown sugar
⅛	teaspoon ground cinnamon
	Pinch ground nutmeg
¼	cup apricot nectar or orange juice
1	17.3-ounce package frozen puff pastry (2 sheets), thawed for 30 minutes
½	cup walnuts, coarsely chopped

✳ In a small saucepan combine apricots, brown sugar, cinnamon, nutmeg, and nectar. Bring to boiling over medium-high heat. Cover; reduce heat to medium-low. Cook for 8–10 minutes or until thickened.

✳ Transfer apricot mixture to food processor or blender. Purée until almost completely smooth, but still with some small pieces; you should have about 1 cup filling. Set filling aside to cool.

✳ Preheat oven to 425°F.

✳ Unroll 1 pastry sheet on lightly floured surface. Spread half the apricot filling over pastry. Cut sheet in half lengthwise; cut each half crosswise into 8 equal strips. Roll up each strip, short end to short end, enclosing filling. Repeat with remaining sheet of pastry and filling, to make a total of 32 roll-ups.

✳ Spoon about ½ teaspoon chopped nuts into each of 32 cups (1¾ x ¾ inch) in mini-muffin pans (3 pans). Place a roll-up, cut-side up, in each cup.

✳ Bake one pan 15–18 minutes or until roll-ups are puffed and golden. Transfer swirls to rack to cool. (While baking one mini-muffin pan, keep other pans refrigerated. Or if you have only one mini-muffin pan, refrigerate other unbaked roll-ups. After baking one batch, rinse pan in cold water to cool, then dry the pan and proceed with the other batches of swirls.)

✳ Serve cookies slightly warm or at room temperature. Makes 32 cookies.

Cookies & Other Petite Confections ✳

White Chocolate Berry Twists

Tired of the same old cookies? Try these five-ingredient wonders—they just may be the best cookies you've tasted. If dark chocolate suits your fancy, use it instead of the white, and take the liberty of using your favorite jam or preserves in place of the raspberry.

> 1 large egg
> 1 tablespoon water
> ½ of a 17.3-ounce package frozen puff pastry (1 sheet), thawed for 30 minutes
> 2 tablespoons raspberry jam
> 2 1-ounce squares white baking chocolate, finely chopped

✳ Preheat oven to 400°F. Mix egg and water in a small bowl with a fork. Set aside.

✳ Unfold pastry on lightly floured surface. Roll out to a 14x10-inch rectangle. Spread with jam. Cut pastry in half lengthwise. Sprinkle one half with white chocolate. Place remaining rectangle over chocolate-topped rectangle, jam-side down. Roll gently with rolling pin to seal.

✳ Cut pastry crosswise into twenty-eight (28) ½-inch strips. Twist strips and place 2 inches apart on greased baking sheet, pressing down ends. Brush with egg mixture.

✳ Bake 10–12 minutes or until golden. Serve warm or at room temperature. Makes 28 twists.

✳ *Cookies & Other Petite Confections*

Sacristan Cookies

Let a platter of these cinnamon–almond cookies take center stage on a holiday dessert buffet table.

½	of a 17.3-ounce package frozen puff pastry (1 sheet), thawed for 30 minutes
¼	cup packed light brown sugar
¼	cup finely chopped slivered almonds
1½	teaspoons ground cinnamon
1	large egg yolk
1	tablespoon water
2	tablespoons powdered sugar

✳ On a lightly floured surface roll out puff pastry to a 12-inch square. Line a baking sheet with parchment paper.

✳ In a small bowl mix brown sugar, almonds, and cinnamon. In a small cup whisk the egg yolk and water.

✳ Brush egg mixture over puff pastry. Sprinkle half the sugar mixture evenly over pastry, then turn pastry over and brush second side with egg mixture. Sprinkle remaining sugar mixture over this side of pastry. Cut into twenty-four (24) ½-inch-wide strips. Take each strip and gently twist from both ends about 4 times.

✳ Place twisted sticks on prepared baking sheets as straight as possible and 1½ inches apart. Refrigerate, loosely covered with plastic wrap, for 30 minutes.

✳ Preheat oven to 350°F. Bake 20 minutes or until puffed and golden. Transfer to a wire rack to cool. Dust the cookies with powdered sugar. Makes about 24 cookies.

Cookies & Other Petite Confections ✳

Date-Walnut Triangles

Cardamom has a spicy-sweet flavor evocative of grapefruit. Used in a range of dishes from Scandinavian baked goods to East Asian curries, it lends an exotic twist to these delicate holiday cookies.

1	cup chopped walnuts
1	8-ounce package chopped dates
¼	cup butter, softened
2	tablespoons all-purpose flour
2	tablespoons sugar
1	teaspoon ground cardamom
1	17.3-ounce package frozen puff pastry (2 sheets), thawed for 30 minutes

✳ Line baking sheets with parchment paper.

✳ Place walnuts and dates in food processor bowl fitted with metal blade. Process until finely chopped. Add butter, flour, sugar, and cardamom; process until well mixed.

✳ Roll out 1 sheet of puff pastry on lightly floured surface into a 10½-inch square. Cut each into nine (9) 3½-inch squares. Repeat with second sheet of puff pastry. Divide date mixture evenly among squares. Starting with one corner, fold each square diagonally in half to form triangle. Seal edges together with fork.

✳ Place triangles onto ungreased large baking sheets. Refrigerate 20 minutes.

✳ Preheat oven to 400°F. Bake pastries 12–15 minutes or until triangles are lightly browned. Transfer to wire rack to cool. Serve warm or room temperature. Makes 18 triangles.

Coconut Palmiers

This cookie began life as a coconut sugar cookie that tasted great, but was more than a little time-consuming. Ironically, this quick variation is far grander in both appearance and taste thanks to the simplicity of flavors and double-swirl design.

1	17.3-ounce package frozen puff pastry (2 sheets), thawed for 30 minutes
4	tablespoons sugar, divided use
1	large egg
1	tablespoon dark rum
¾	cup sweetened flake coconut, very finely chopped
1	teaspoon grated lime zest

✳ Preheat oven to 400°F. Line baking sheets with parchment paper.

✳ Unfold 1 of the pastry sheets on a surface sprinkled with 2 tablespoons sugar; roll out sheet to a 16x12-inch rectangle. Repeat with the second sheet.

✳ Combine egg and rum in a small cup. Brush pastry sheets with half of mixture.

✳ In a small bowl combine chopped coconut, lime zest, and remaining 2 tablespoons sugar; sprinkle over pastry sheets. Starting at each short end, roll pastry up tightly, jelly roll–fashion, to meet in center. (The shape of the roll resembles a scroll.) Brush with remaining egg mixture.

✳ Cut each roll into ½-inch-thick slices. Place 2 inches apart on prepared sheets.

✳ Bake for 8–10 minutes or until palmiers are golden. Makes about 4 dozen palmiers.

Chocolate Peanut Butter Cups

These delightful mini-tart cups hold just the right amount of gooey chocolate-peanut butter-marshmallow filling.

½	of a 17.3-ounce package frozen puff pastry (1 sheet), thawed for 30 minutes
6	tablespoons creamy peanut butter
⅓	cup semisweet chocolate chips
1	cup miniature marshmallows

✳ Preheat oven to 400°F.

✳ Unfold pastry on lightly floured surface. Roll out to an 18x9-inch rectangle. Cut into 18 3-inch squares. Press squares into 3-inch muffin-pan cups.

✳ Place 1 teaspoon peanut butter in center of each. Top each with 3–4 chocolate chips and about 4 marshmallows.

✳ Bake 10–12 minutes or until golden. Cool in pan on wire rack 10 minutes. Remove from pan and cool completely on wire rack. Makes 18 pastries.

Chocolate Raspberry Pastry Cups

You can take these bite-size chocolate treats everywhere and anywhere—they fit right in, whether at a sophisticated bash or a casual backyard birthday party. Your guests will likely want more than one, so consider doubling the recipe if more than a dozen people are expected.

½   of a 17.3-ounce package frozen puff pastry (1 sheet), thawed for 30 minutes
1   large egg, lightly beaten
½   cup heavy whipping cream
1½ teaspoons powdered sugar
½   teaspoon vanilla extract
1   13-ounce jar chocolate hazelnut spread
1   pint fresh raspberries
     Fresh mint leaves for garnish

✳ Preheat oven to 375°F. Spray the cups of a 3-inch muffin pan with cooking spray.

✳ Unfold pastry sheet on a lightly floured surface. Roll out to a 12x9-inch rectangle. Cut into twelve (12) 3-inch squares. Press squares into prepared muffin pan cups. Brush only the sides of the pastry cups with egg. Prick the bottom of the pastry cups with fork.

✳ Bake for 10–12 minutes or until golden. Cool in pan on wire rack for 10 minutes. Remove pastry cups from pan and cool completely.

✳ Place cream, sugar, and vanilla in a medium bowl. Beat with mixer at high speed until stiff.

✳ Spoon a rounded tablespoon chocolate hazelnut spread in each pastry cup. Top each with 3–4 raspberries. Spoon a heaping teaspoon whipped cream on top of the raspberries. Garnish with mint leaves. Serve immediately. Makes 12 pastries.

Fudge-y Brownie Mini Tarts

Here all-American brownies get a French twist—but without any added fuss or muss. They'll satisfy your cravings for both a chocolate fix and a delicate pastry in one bite.

4	1-ounce squares unsweetened baking chocolate
¼	cup (½ stick) butter
¾	cup sugar
2	large eggs
1	teaspoon vanilla extract
2	tablespoons all-purpose flour
½	of a 17.3-ounce package frozen puff pastry (1 sheet), thawed for 30 minutes
2	tablespoons powdered sugar

✳ Preheat oven to 400°F.

✳ In a large microwavable bowl microwave chocolate and butter on high for 1 minute or until butter is melted. Stir until chocolate is completely melted. Mix in the sugar, eggs, vanilla, and flour until well blended.

✳ Unfold pastry sheet on lightly floured surface. Roll out to a 15 x 12-inch rectangle. Cut into 20 3-inch squares. Press 1 square onto bottom and up the side of each of 20 2½-inch muffin cups. Fill each with 1 tablespoon of the chocolate mixture.

✳ Bake 15–20 minutes or until pastry is golden brown. Remove from muffin pans. Cool on wire racks. Sprinkle with powdered sugar. Makes 20 mini tarts.

Cherry Purses with Chocolate Sauce

Accompanied by a ready-made but still decadent chocolate sauce, these tart cherry-filled purses are an exquisite combination of flavors.

1½	cups fresh or canned tart cherries, pitted and coarsely chopped
¼	cup cherry preserves
1	tablespoon cherry liqueur or cherry brandy
1	17.3-ounce package frozen puff pastry (2 sheets), thawed for 30 minutes
1	tablespoon sugar
1	teaspoon ground cinnamon
2	tablespoons milk
1	cup jarred premium chocolate fudge ice cream topping, warmed

✻ Preheat oven to 400°F. Line baking sheet with parchment paper.

✻ In a medium bowl combine the cherries, preserves, and liqueur.

✻ Unfold 1 pastry sheet on lightly floured surface. Cut pastry in half lengthwise. Roll out each piece to a 15 x 5-inch rectangle. Cut each rectangle crosswise to make 3 5-inch squares. Repeat with remaining pastry sheet.

✻ Spoon cherry mixture into center of pastry squares. Fold corners to center on top of filling and twist tightly to seal. Place pastries on baking sheet.

✻ Mix sugar and cinnamon. Brush pastries with milk and sprinkle with sugar mixture.

✻ Bake 13–16 minutes or until golden. Serve warm with warm chocolate sauce. Makes 12 pastries.

Petite Pain au Chocolat

Ooh la la—these are little packages of chocoholic heaven. You can vary the chocolate—bittersweet, white, milk, your choice—all with great success.

1	17.3-ounce package frozen puff pastry (2 sheets), thawed for 30 minutes
1½	cups semisweet chocolate chips, divided use
1	large egg, lightly beaten
2	tablespoons butter
1	cup powdered sugar
2	tablespoons hot water

✳ Preheat oven to 350° F. Line 2 baking sheets with parchment paper.

✳ Unfold 1 pastry sheet on lightly floured surface. Roll out to make a 10-inch square. Cut into 4 squares.

✳ Place 2 tablespoons chocolate chips in center of each square. Brush edges lightly with beaten egg and fold squares to form triangles. Press edges to seal. Place on prepared baking sheet about 2 inches apart. Repeat with remaining pastry sheet. Place pastries on prepared sheets. Brush top of each pastry with beaten egg.

✳ Bake for 15–17 minutes or until puffed and golden. Cool on baking sheets for 2 minutes; remove to wire racks to cool completely.

✳ In a small, uncovered, microwave-safe bowl melt remaining ½ cup chocolate chips and butter on high power for 30 seconds; stir. If necessary, microwave at additional 10- to 15-second intervals, stirring just until chips are melted. Stir in powdered sugar. Add water, stirring until icing is smooth, adding additional water, if necessary. Drizzle icing over pastries. Makes 8 pastries.

Mini Berry Puffs with Lemon-Honey Cream

The bright, acidic flavor of lemon accentuates the delicate, perfume-y sweetness of berries in this mouth-watering rendition of cream puffs.

I	17.3-ounce package frozen puff pastry (2 sheets), thawed for 30 minutes
1/3	cup seedless raspberry jam
1 1/2	cups blueberries, divided use
2	tablespoons fresh lemon juice
2/3	cup chilled heavy whipping cream
2	teaspoons finely grated fresh lemon zest
I	tablespoon honey
I	cup raspberries
	Powdered sugar for dusting

✳ Preheat oven to 425°F. Line a baking sheet with parchment paper.

✳ Unfold pastry sheet on a lightly floured surface. Cut 9 squares from sheet with a long sharp knife. Repeat with second sheet.

✳ Arrange squares on prepared baking sheets and lightly prick centers a few times with a fork. Bake in middle of oven until puffed and golden brown, 15–18 minutes. Transfer to a rack and cool.

✳ While the pastry bakes, purée the jam, ½ cup of the blueberries, and lemon juice in a blender or food processor until smooth. Transfer to a bowl and set aside.

✳ In a small bowl beat the cream, zest, and honey until it just holds stiff peaks.

✳ Split each pastry square in half horizontally and make a sandwich with about 2 tablespoons cream. Spread some purée on top of each pastry, leaving a ¼-inch border. Decoratively arrange some blueberries on top and sift some powdered sugar over berries. Makes 18 puff pastries.

✔ **Cook's Notes:** ✳ *The berry purée can be made 2 days ahead and chilled, covered;* ✳ *The lemon cream can be made 8 hours ahead and chilled, covered.*

Apricot & Gingered Mascarpone Napoleons

French napoleons go nouveau with the benefit of apricots, ginger, and mascarpone cheese. Several sub-stitutions can be made here: canned apricots work quite well if fresh are not up to snuff, and an 8-ounce package of cream cheese may be used if mascarpone is unavailable.

$\frac{1}{2}$	of a 17.3-ounce package frozen puff pastry (1 sheet), thawed for 30 minutes
$1\frac{1}{2}$	pounds apricots, pitted and quartered
1	8-ounce container mascarpone cheese, room temperature
1	tablespoon finely chopped crystallized ginger, or to taste
$2\frac{1}{2}$	tablespoons sugar
$\frac{3}{4}$	teaspoon vanilla
	Powdered sugar for dusting

✳ On a lightly floured surface roll out pastry to a 15x12-inch rectangle. Halve pastry lengthwise with a pastry wheel or large knife to form two 15x6-inch strips. Cut each strip crosswise into 7 equal rectangles (for a total of 14). Arrange rectangles in 1 layer on a large baking sheet lined with parchment paper. Chill, loosely covered with plastic wrap, for 20 minutes.

✳ Preheat oven to 400°F.

✳ While pastry is chilling, chop $\frac{1}{2}$ cup of the apricots and stir together with mascar-pone, ginger, sugar, and vanilla. Chill filling, covered.

✳ Place a sheet of parchment paper atop pastry. Place a second baking sheet directly on top of the baking sheet containing the parchment-topped pastry (to prevent much rising). Bake pastry in upper third of oven until golden and cooked through, 15–18 minutes. Remove top baking sheet carefully and transfer baked pastry to rack to cool completely.

✳ Spread filling over 7 of the pastry rectangles and top with half of remaining quar-tered apricots, overlapping if needed. Dust with powdered sugar. Cover apricots with remaining pastry rectangles and top with remaining apricots, overlapping if needed. Dust with powdered sugar. Makes 7 napoleons.

✳ *Cookies & Other Petite Confections*

Fresh Mango Napoleons

What better way to celebrate than with a fresh, tropical take on a time-honored classic?

I   8-ounce package cream cheese, softened

¾   cup powdered sugar, divided use

I   teaspoon vanilla extract

¼   teaspoon ground allspice

⅔   cup chilled whipping cream

½   of a 17.3-ounce package frozen puff pastry (I sheet), thawed for 30 minutes

½   cup pineapple or apricot preserves

3   firm-ripe mangoes, peeled, pitted, and diced

    Fresh mint sprigs

❋ Preheat oven to 375°F. Using electric mixer, beat cream cheese, ¼ cup powdered sugar, vanilla, and allspice in medium bowl until fluffy. Using same beaters, beat whipping cream in another medium bowl until peaks form. Fold whipped cream into cream cheese mixture in 3 additions. Cover mousse and refrigerate.

❋ Roll out pastry sheet on lightly floured surface to a 14x10 and ½-inch rectangle. Cut sheet into twelve (12) 3½-inch squares. Pierce squares all over with fork. Sift ¼ cup powdered sugar over squares.

❋ Place squares on baking sheet lined with parchment paper. Bake 10–12 minutes until puffed and golden. Using metal spatula, flatten squares and continue baking until crisp and brown, about 5 minutes longer. Cool pastry squares on sheet.

❋ Heat preserves in small saucepan until just melted. Transfer to medium bowl. Add diced mango and toss to coat.

❋ Place 6 pastry squares on work surface. Spread each with ¼ cup mousse. Top with about ½ cup mango mixture. Cover with remaining pastry squares. Dust napoleons with remaining ¼ cup powdered sugar. Top each with mint sprig. Place napoleons on plates. Makes 6 servings.

Cookies & Other Petite Confections ❋

Crème Fraîche-Raspberry Puffs

These delicate puffs are a balanced blend of beautiful ingredients, combining fruit, fluff, and puff in a single bite. The simple filling of crème fraîche allows each of the elements to shine through.

½	of a 17.3-ounce package frozen puff pastry (1 sheet), thawed for 30 minutes
¾	cup crème fraîche
2½	tablespoons sugar
2	cups fresh raspberries
2	tablespoons powdered sugar

✻ Put oven rack in upper third of oven. Preheat oven to 400°F. Line a baking sheet with parchment paper.

✻ Unfold pastry sheet on a lightly floured surface and roll out to a 10-inch square. Cut into 4 squares.

✻ Bake pastry squares 15–18 minutes on an ungreased baking sheet until golden brown. Transfer pastry to a rack and cool completely, then cut pastry horizontally into 2 layers.

✻ Stir together crème fraîche and sugar until sugar is dissolved.

✻ Just before serving, put bottom half of pastry on a plate and top with crème fraîche and raspberries, letting some berries spill onto plate. Cover with top half of pastry and dust with powdered sugar. Makes 4 servings.

✻ *Cookies & Other Petite Confections*

These traditional Portuguese pastries are all about texture—the rich, creamy, lemon-accented filling is simply sublime atop the crispy, puffy pastry bottoms. Served with afternoon coffee, they're even more delicious.

1	17.3-ounce package frozen puff pastry (2 sheets), thawed for 30 minutes
2	tablespoons butter, melted
1	cup sugar
2	tablespoons all-purpose flour
2½	cups heavy cream
1¼	teaspoons grated lemon zest
8	large egg yolks
¼	teaspoon salt
1	teaspoon vanilla
1	tablespoon powdered sugar
½	teaspoon cinnamon

✳ Gently unfold 1 pastry sheet and cut along folds, forming 3 equal strips (each about 9 x 3 inches). Stack pieces and cut stack lengthwise into twelve (12) ¼-inch-wide strips, each strip 3 layers thick. Repeat with remaining pastry sheet.

✳ Turn each triple strip on its side (cut-side up) and coil tightly to form a flat 2- to 2½-inch-wide spiral. On a lightly floured surface, press spiral with palm to flatten into a 3-inch round.

✳ Lightly brush 2 12-cup muffin cups (about ⅓ cup each) with melted butter. Place each round in a muffin cup and press into bottom and side, lining cup to within ⅛ inch of top.

✳ Preheat oven to 450°F. In a medium-size heavy saucepan whisk the sugar and flour. Whisk in cream, lemon zest, egg yolks, and salt. Cook over medium heat, whisking constantly, until custard just begins to bubble, about 10 minutes. Whisk in vanilla. Transfer custard to a bowl and cool, whisking occasionally, until just warm, about 15 minutes. Fill pastry cups with custard, about 2 tablespoons each.

✳ Bake tarts in upper third of oven until pastry is deep golden, 10–12 minutes. (Filling may brown slightly.)

✳ Cool tarts in pans on a rack for 10 minutes. Carefully lift tarts from pans using a small offset spatula or dull knife. Sift powdered sugar, then cinnamon, over tarts and serve warm or at room temperature. Makes 24 small tarts.

Cookies & Other Petite Confections ✳

Pineapple-Rum Tartlets

You won't believe such a sophisticated dessert can result from such common ingredients. The rum-flavored filling teases out the deep tropical flavors of the fresh pineapple. Purchasing pre-trimmed, pre-cored pineapple in the produce section simplifies the tartlets considerably.

I   17.3-ounce package frozen puff pastry (2 sheets), thawed for 30 minutes
I   large pineapple, trimmed, peeled, cored, but left whole
I   cup premium caramel ice cream topping
2   tablespoons dark rum
I   teaspoon ground ginger
I   large egg yolk
I   tablespoon milk
    Vanilla ice cream

✳ Roll out I of the pastry sheets on a lightly floured surface to a 12-inch square. Using a small plate as guide, cut four 5- to 5½-inch rounds from square. Repeat with second pastry sheet. Transfer rounds to 2 baking sheets lined with parchment paper. Refrigerate, loosely covered with plastic wrap, for at least 30 minutes.

✳ Preheat oven to 350°F. Place pineapple in 13 x 9 x 2-inch glass baking dish. In a small bowl mix the caramel topping, rum, and ginger. Pour caramel over pineapple, turning to coat. Roast until tender, basting often with sauce and adding more water by tablespoonfuls if sauce becomes thick, about I hour 15 minutes. Cool.

✳ Increase oven temperature to 375°F. Whisk the egg yolk and milk in a small cup. Transfer pineapple to work surface, scraping any sauce back into dish. Cut pineapple crosswise into 8 thick rounds. Place I pineapple round in center of each pastry round. Brush pineapple with the reserved sauce. Brush pastry edges with egg glaze.

✳ Bake tartlets until pastry is brown, about 22–25 minutes. Meanwhile, reheat caramel sauce from roasted pineapple in a small saucepan over low heat until just warm. Top each tartlet with scoop of vanilla ice cream; drizzle with warm sauce and serve. Makes 8 tartlets.

✔ **Cook's Note:** ✳ *The unbaked pastry rounds may be prepared and refrigerated up to 1 day ahead;* ✳ *The roasted pineapple can be made 1 day ahead. Chill until cold, then cover and keep chilled.*

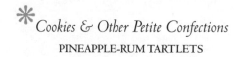

Cookies & Other Petite Confections

Apple-Cranberry Turnovers

Forget the fussiness—these tart-sweet turnovers are a pleasure to prepare.

3	tablespoons apple jelly
I	large tart-sweet apple, peeled, cored, and cut into ¼-inch pieces
⅓	cup dried cranberries
I	tablespoon cornstarch
⅛	teaspoon cinnamon
½	of a 17.3-ounce package frozen puff pastry (I sheet), thawed for 30 minutes
I	large egg, lightly beaten
2	tablespoons cold unsalted butter, cut into bits
I	tablespoon sugar

✳ Put oven rack in lower third of oven and preheat oven to 400°F.

✳ Place the jelly in a medium microwaveable bowl. Microwave on high 30 seconds. Stir in apple, cranberries, cornstarch, and cinnamon.

✳ Roll out pastry on a lightly floured surface into a 12 x 9-inch rectangle. Cut into 6 squares. Divide apple mixture among squares, leaving a 1-inch border, and lightly brush egg on border. Dot filling with butter. Fold each pastry into a triangle, enclosing filling, and crimp edges with a fork. Cut 2 small steam vents in top of each turnover.

✳ Place turnovers on baking sheet lined with parchment paper. Brush tops lightly with more egg and sprinkle with sugar.

✳ Bake 18–20 minutes until puffed and golden. Cool until warm but not hot, about 20 minutes. Makes 6 turnovers.

Cookies & Other Petite Confections ✳

Cherry-Almond Tartlets

Homemade desserts are always a pleasure. Boasting a triple cherry-almond filling, these simple tartlets will enliven any summer soiree.

$\frac{1}{2}$	cup cherry preserves
$\frac{1}{2}$	teaspoon almond extract
I	cup chopped, fresh, pitted cherries
$\frac{3}{4}$	cup dried tart cherries, coarsely chopped
$\frac{1}{2}$	of a 17.3-ounce package frozen puff pastry (I sheet), thawed for 30 minutes
I	large egg yolk, lightly beaten
$\frac{1}{4}$	cup sliced almonds, toasted

✳ Preheat oven to 400°F. Line baking sheet with parchment paper.

✳ Mix jam and almond extract in small saucepan. Transfer $\frac{1}{4}$ cup jam mixture to medium bowl. Add fresh cherries and dried cherries; toss to combine.

✳ Unfold pastry sheet on a lightly floured surface. Roll out to a 10-inch square. Using 3-inch-diameter cookie cutter, cut 9 rounds from puff pastry; discard trimmings.

✳ Arrange rounds on prepared baking sheet, spacing evenly. Pierce center of pastries with fork, leaving $\frac{1}{4}$-inch edge unpierced. Brush edges with beaten egg yolk. Mound fruit mixture in center of pastries, pressing to compact.

✳ Bake until golden brown, about 22–25 minutes.

✳ In a saucepan heat remaining jam mixture over medium-high heat until just beginning to boil. Brush jam mixture over filling and pastry edges. Sprinkle with almonds. Transfer tarts to rack and cool completely. Makes 9 tartlets.

✳ *Cookies & Other Petite Confections*

CHERRY-ALMOND TARTLETS

Brandied Pear Tarts

A splash of brandy gives delicate puff pastry and succulent pears an appealing French accent.

1   17.3-ounce package frozen puff pastry (2 sheets), thawed for 30 minutes

2   large Bosc pears, peeled, halved, cored, cut lengthwise into ⅛-inch-thick slices

2   tablespoons (¼ stick) unsalted butter, melted

4   tablespoons sugar

1   pint vanilla ice cream

3   tablespoons brandy

✳ Preheat oven to 425°F.

✳ Roll out 1 pastry sheet on lightly floured work surface to a 9x13-inch rectangle. Using 6-inch plate as aid, cut out 2 rounds. Repeat rolling and cutting with second pastry sheet, forming 4 rounds total.

✳ Place rounds on a large heavy baking sheet, spacing apart. Using 1 pear half for each tart, fan out pear slices in center of each round. Brush tarts with melted butter; sprinkle each with 1 tablespoon sugar.

✳ Bake until pears are tender and pastry is golden, about 20–22 minutes. Transfer tarts to plates. Top each with ice cream and drizzle with brandy. Makes 4 servings.

Plum Pastry Tarts with Cardamom Sugar

The bright, sweet-tart flavor of fresh plums, complemented by the warm, spicy-sweet flavor of cardamom, makes for easily assembled tarts with seasonal panache.

2	tablespoons sugar
¼	teaspoon ground cardamom
½	of a 17.3-ounce package frozen puff pastry (1 sheet), thawed for 30 minutes
8	large plums, halved, pitted, and cut into ¼-inch-thick slices
⅓	cup plum jam
1	pint vanilla ice cream (optional)

✳ Preheat oven to 400°F. Line a baking sheet with parchment paper.

✳ Mix the sugar and cardamom in a small cup.

✳ On a lightly floured surface roll out pastry to a 12-inch square. Cut pastry into four 6-inch squares.

✳ Arrange pastry squares on an prepared baking sheet and fold edges in on all sides to form ½-inch borders, leaving corners unfolded. Form points at corners by twisting ends and pressing them gently onto baking sheet. On pastry arrange plum slices, overlapping them slightly, in rows. Sprinkle with cardamom-sugar mixture.

✳ Bake tarts in middle of oven until pastry is golden brown, about 20–25 minutes. Cool tarts on a rack. In a small saucepan set over low heat melt the jam. Brush melted jam over tarts. Serve tarts warm with ice cream. Makes 4 tarts.

✳ *Cookies & Other Petite Confections*

PB & J Napoleons

It's easy to stereotype peanut butter and jelly as kiddie cuisine, but this very grown-up interpretation—puff pastry, a peanut butter-caramel cream, and berries—proves otherwise.

½ of a 17.3-ounce package frozen puff pastry (1 sheet), thawed for 30 minutes

1 8-ounce package cream cheese, softened

½ cup creamy peanut butter

1 cup jarred premium caramel ice cream topping

3 cups fresh raspberries or blackberries
   Powdered sugar

✳ Line 2 large baking sheets with parchment paper.

✳ Roll out pastry on lightly floured surface to 15 x 12-inch rectangle. Cut crosswise into three 12 x 5-inch strips. Transfer pastry strips to prepared baking sheets, spacing evenly. Refrigerate, loosely covered, 20 minutes.

✳ Preheat oven to 400°F. Pierce pastry with fork. Bake until golden, about 15–18 minutes. Transfer baking sheets to racks; cool.

✳ Using electric mixer, beat cream cheese, peanut butter, and ½ cup of the caramel topping in medium bowl until smooth.

✳ Place 1 pastry strip on work surface. Spread with one-fourth of the peanut butter cream. Arrange half of berries in single layer over peanut butter cream. Spread second pastry strip with one-fourth of the peanut butter cream; place pastry, peanut-butter-cream-side down, atop berries. Spread top of second pastry strip with one-fourth of the peanut butter cream. Arrange remaining berries in single layer over. Spread remaining pastry strip with remaining peanut butter cream. Place pastry, peanut-butter -cream-side down, atop berries.

✳ Using serrated knife, cut pastry crosswise into 8 equal pieces. Sift powdered sugar over. Place napoleons on plates. Drizzle reserved caramel mixture around napoleons. Makes 8 servings.

Cookies & Other Petite Confections ✳

Pineapple-Lime Triangles

Serving a dessert this decadent doesn't require a special event—Tuesday night is occasion enough.

½	of a 17.3-ounce package frozen puff pastry (1 sheet), thawed for 30 minutes
1	large egg yolk
2	tablespoons heavy cream (or milk)
¼	cup pineapple preserves
1	teaspoon fresh lime juice
1	teaspoon grated lime zest
4	1-ounce white chocolate baking squares, coarsely chopped (about 6 tablespoons)
2	tablespoons sugar

✳ Preheat oven to 400°F. Line a baking sheet with parchment paper.

✳ On lightly floured board roll out pastry sheet to an 11-inch square. Cut into 4 squares. In small bowl beat together egg yolk and cream. Brush eggwash along 2 adjacent edges of each square.

✳ In a small cup combine the jam, lime juice, and lime zest. Divide white chocolate among pastry squares, placing slightly below center. Top each with 1 tablespoon jam mixture. Fold pastry to enclose filling and form triangle. Using tines of fork, press edges well to seal. Place on large parchment paper or foil-lined baking sheet; set in freezer 20 minutes.

✳ Brush each triangle with remaining egg wash; sprinkle evenly with sugar. Bake 15–17 minutes until golden and puffed. Makes 4 pastries.

✳ *Cookies & Other Petite Confections*

Fresh Fig & Honey Purses

Honey enhances the lush, summer sweetness of ripe figs. If you like, you can substitute fresh or dried lavender for the rosemary.

16	fresh figs, stemmed and diced
¼	cup honey
2	teaspoons chopped fresh rosemary
1	17.3-ounce package frozen puff pastry (2 sheets), thawed for 30 minutes
2	tablespoons whole milk
1	tablespoon granulated sugar

✳ Position rack in center of oven. Preheat oven to 400°F.

✳ Line a baking sheet with parchment paper.

✳ In a medium bowl combine figs, honey, and rosemary. On a lightly floured surface, lay flat 1 sheet of puff pastry. Cut pastry in half lengthwise. Using a rolling pin, roll out each pastry sheet to a 15 x 5-inch rectangle. Cut each rectangle crosswise into thirds, forming 6 squares total. Repeat with second sheet of puff pastry.

✳ Place a generous spoonful of the fig mixture onto center of each square. Fold corners of pastry into center and pinch ends together, twisting to seal. Arrange pastries on prepared baking sheet. Brush pastries with milk and sprinkle with sugar.

✳ Bake for 14–17 minutes or until golden. Serve warm. Makes 12 pastries.

Blueberry Turnovers

Bursting with blueberries, these handheld pastries taste like deep-dish blueberry pie but are much easier to make.

1	17.3-ounce package frozen puff pastry (2 sheets), thawed for 30 minutes
½	cup blueberry preserves
2	tablespoons cornstarch
2	tablespoons brown sugar
½	teaspoon grated lemon zest
1	cup fresh blueberries or frozen (thawed) blueberries
½	teaspoon pure vanilla extract
1	large egg
2	teaspoons water
2	tablespoons sugar

✱ Lightly flour a work surface. Roll out each puff pastry sheet to a 12-inch square. Cover with plastic wrap and chill 20 minutes.

✱ Preheat oven to 375°F.

✱ In a small mixing bowl stir together the preserves, cornstarch, brown sugar, and lemon zest. Fold in the blueberries and vanilla and put the mixture in the refrigerator. Using a sharp knife, cut each puff pastry sheet into four 6-inch squares.

✱ Whisk egg and water in small cup. Lay a pastry square on a work surface and brush the edges with egg wash. In the center of the square, place 2 heaping tablespoons of the blueberry filling. Brush the edges of the pastry square with egg wash and fold it in half to create a triangle. Carefully press the edges together to seal them well with fork tines.

✱ Transfer turnovers to baking sheet lined with parchment paper. Brush the turnovers with the egg wash and sprinkle with the 2 tablespoons sugar.

✱ Bake turnovers 20–25 minutes until golden brown. Serve warm or let cool to room temperature. Makes 8 turnovers.

✱ *Cookies & Other Petite Confections*

Raspberry–Cream Cheese Turnovers

Gazing into my crystal ball, I predict you will make these creamy, raspberry-filled foldovers for countless occasions, including my favorite: an afternoon tea break.

½	of a 17.3-ounce package frozen puff pastry (1 sheet), thawed for 30 minutes
4	ounces cream cheese (half of an 8-ounce package), softened
1	large egg yolk
½	cup powdered sugar
½	teaspoon vanilla extract
1	teaspoon grated lemon zest
1	large egg
2	teaspoons water
1	cup raspberries
2	teaspoons sugar

✳ On a lightly floured surface roll out the pastry sheet to an 11-inch square. Refrigerate, loosely covered with plastic wrap, 30 minutes.

✳ Preheat oven to 375°F.

✳ In a medium bowl mix the cream cheese, egg yolk, powdered sugar, vanilla extract, and lemon zest with electric mixer until blended and smooth. Make an egg wash by whisking together the egg and water in a small bowl.

✳ Cut the puff pastry into 9 squares.

✳ Lay a square of pastry on a work surface and brush the edge with egg wash. In the center of the pastry, place 1 tablespoon of cheese filling and 3 raspberries. Brush the edge of a second square of pastry with egg wash, place it on top of the filling and carefully press the edges together to seal them well.

✳ Place pockets 1 inch apart on a baking sheet lined with parchment paper. Brush the top surface of each turnover with egg wash; sprinkle with sugar.

✳ Bake 20–25 minutes until golden brown. Makes 9 turnovers.

Cookies & Other Petite Confections ✳

Fresh Fruit–Filled Cream Horns

These light and airy pastries will literally melt in your mouth. To pipe in the whipped cream, fill a large zipper-top bag with the cream and snip off one of the corners. Enjoy varying the fruits according to what's in season.

½   of a 17.3-ounce package frozen puff pastry (I sheet), thawed for 30 minutes

I   large egg

I   teaspoon water

3   tablespoons powdered sugar, divided use

I   cup heavy whipping cream

I   tablespoon sugar

2   cups bite-size fresh fruit such as Clementine sections, blueberries, diced kiwi, or diced strawberries

✻ Grease 8 cream horn metal cones. Unfold the puff pastry sheet onto a lightly floured surface. Cut pastry into ½-inch-wide strips. Starting at the point of the cone, wind the pastry around the cone, overlapping the layers slightly to cover the cone with a spiral of pastry. Place, seam-side down, on a parchment-paper-lined baking sheet and freeze 30 minutes.

✻ Preheat oven to 400°F.

✻ Whisk the egg with the water in a small cup. Lightly brush the pastry cones with the egg wash. Sift some powdered sugar all over the puff pastry cones. Bake 18–20 minutes or until golden brown. Transfer sheet to a wire rack.

✻ Let pastry horns cool on the metal cones. When cool, carefully remove the metal cones.

✻ In a medium bowl whip cream with the I tablespoon sugar using an electric mixer set on high until stiff peaks form. Just before serving, pipe the whipped cream into the pastry, then place it on a dessert plate. Garnish the cream horns with cascading cut-up fruit, then dust with more powdered sugar. Makes 8 cream horns.

✻ *Cookies & Other Petite Confections*

FRESH FRUIT–FILLED CREAM HORNS

Cheddar cheese is a common, and very tasty, accompaniment to New England versions of apple pie. The sharp, nutty bite of cheese together with the perfumed sweetness of tender apples is a combination you simply must try. Here it is made even more appealing in handheld form.

2	Golden Delicious apples, peeled, cored, and chopped
2	teaspoons fresh lemon juice
¼	cup packed light brown sugar
½	teaspoon ground cinnamon
	Pinch ground nutmeg
	Pinch salt
2	tablespoons butter
2	tablespoons all-purpose flour
½	of a 17.3-ounce package frozen puff pastry (1 sheet), thawed for 30 minutes
1	cup diced sharp Cheddar cheese (about 4 ounces)
1	large egg
1	tablespoon water

✳ In a bowl toss the apples with the lemon juice. Add the brown sugar, cinnamon, nutmeg, and salt; toss to combine.

✳ Melt the butter in a large skillet set over medium-high heat. Add apple mixture and cook and stir 7–10 minutes until apple juices release and apples are slightly softened. Sprinkle flour over mixture. Cook for about 2 minutes. Remove from heat and cool.

✳ Preheat the oven to 425°F. Line a baking sheet with parchment paper.

✳ On a lightly floured surface roll out the pastry sheet to a 12 x 10-inch rectangle. Cut pastry sheet into 6 squares.

✳ Add the diced cheese to cooled apple mixture. Divide the apple mixture in the center of each pastry square, leaving a 1-inch border along the long sides. Carefully fold into triangle shape, crimp the ends together with fork to seal, and place on the prepared baking sheet.

✳ In a small bowl beat together the egg and water to make an egg wash. Lightly brush the outside of each square with the egg wash. Using a sharp knife, make a small slit in the top of each triangle.

✳ Bake 20–24 minutes until puffed and golden brown. Remove from oven. Cool slightly. Serve warm. Makes 6 hand pies.

Cookies & Other Petite Confections ✳

White Chocolate Orange Pastries

The lighter-than-air quality of puff pastry, along with an orange-accented white chocolate filling, makes every bite of these confections an exceptional treat. Both the pastry squares and the pastry cream may be prepared a day ahead of time and then assembled later.

½	of a 17.3-ounce package frozen puff pastry (I sheet), thawed for 30 minutes
I	large egg white, lightly beaten with fork until frothy
2	tablespoons turbinado ("raw") sugar
⅓	cup granulated sugar
¼	cup all-purpose flour
¼	teaspoon salt
2	cups half and half
2	ounces white chocolate or white baking squares, chopped
4	large egg yolks, beaten slightly with fork
I	teaspoon vanilla extract
⅓	cup whipping cream
⅓	cup orange marmalade

✻ Preheat the oven to 400°F. Line a baking sheet with parchment paper.

✻ Unfold pastry on a lightly floured surface. Lightly brush pastry with egg white. Sprinkle with raw sugar. Cut the sheet of puff pastry into 25 squares. Place squares 2 inches apart on prepared baking sheet.

✻ Bake pastry squares 12–14 minutes or until golden. Transfer to wire racks and cool.

✻ In a medium-size heavy saucepan combine the sugar, flour, and salt. Gradually stir in half and half and white chocolate. Cook and stir over medium heat until thickened and bubbly. Cook and stir for I minute more.

✻ Gradually stir about half of the hot mixture into a small bowl containing the beaten egg yolks. Return all of the egg yolk mixture to the saucepan. Bring to a gentle boil. Reduce heat; cook and stir for 2 minutes. Remove from heat. Stir in vanilla. Cover surface of pastry cream with plastic wrap. Cool just until warm without stirring (about I½ hours).

✻ Beat whipping cream in a small bowl with an electric mixer on medium-high speed until soft peaks form. Beat in marmalade just until combined. Fold whipped orange

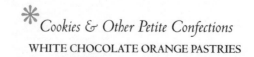

Cookies & Other Petite Confections

cream into the warm pastry cream. Cover and chill for at least 1 hour or up to overnight.

＊ To assemble, split pastry squares into two layers. Pipe cream mixture onto bottom pastry layers using a pastry bag fitted with a $\frac{1}{2}$-inch star or plain tip, or spoon cream mixture onto bottom pastry layers. Add pastry tops. Arrange pastries on a platter. Makes 25 pastries.

Peaches & Cream Packets

Tender and not too sweet, these pastries fall somewhere between a turnover and a danish. Though they're meant for dessert, they also make a very special breakfast.

1	17.3-ounce package frozen puff pastry (2 sheets), thawed for 30 minutes
1	large egg, separated
1	cup ricotta cheese
¼	cup sugar
2	tablespoons all-purpose flour
¼	teaspoon ground cinnamon
½	cup peach preserves
3	cups fresh or frozen (thawed) sliced peaches

✳ Preheat oven to 400°F. Line 2 baking sheets with parchment paper.

✳ Unfold pastry sheets on lightly floured surface. Cut sheets along the fold lines, making 6 pieces total. Cut 4 of the strips crosswise into thirds, creating 12 squares total. Place 6 squares on each of the two prepared baking sheets.

✳ Slice each of the 2 remaining pastry pieces crosswise into 24 strips, for a total of 48 strips. In a small bowl whisk egg white with a fork until frothy. With pastry brush, lightly brush egg white onto pastry squares. Place thin strips around edges of squares to make border (you will need 4 strips per square).

✳ Place one of the baking sheets in the refrigerator. Place the other sheet in oven and bake 10 minutes until pale golden. Transfer sheet to cooling rack. Repeat with second sheet of pastry.

✳ While squares are baking, in small bowl beat together egg yolk, ricotta cheese, sugar, flour, and cinnamon. Spoon generous tablespoon of ricotta mixture into center of each square.

✳ Return both sheets to oven and bake 10–12 minutes more or until cheese mixture is set.

✳ Meanwhile, melt preserves in small saucepan set over low heat. Once packets have been removed from the oven, top each with peach slices and brush with preserves. Return sheets to oven for 2 minutes to warm peaches and glaze. Serve packets slightly warm. Makes 12 packets.

Cookies & Other Petite Confections

Normandy Apple Tartlets

Let the snowflakes dance outside—these traditional French apple tarts will both warm and delight.

1	17.3-ounce package frozen puff pastry (2 sheets), thawed for 30 minutes
4	teaspoons all-purpose flour
3	Granny Smith apples
2	tablespoons butter, melted
8	teaspoons sugar
¾	cup crème fraîche or sour cream

✳ Preheat oven to 400°F. Line a baking sheet with parchment paper.

✳ Unfold one pastry sheet on lightly floured surface. Cut four 4-inch rounds from sheet. Transfer to prepared baking sheet. Prick pastry with fork. Repeat with second sheet for 4 more rounds. Sprinkle each with ½ teaspoon flour.

✳ Peel, core, and thinly slice apples. Arrange slices in single layer on rounds. Brush apples with melted butter. Sprinkle each with 1 teaspoon sugar.

✳ Bake 22–25 minutes or until pastry is golden and apples begin to caramelize lightly around edge. Serve warm or room temperature with crème fraîche or sour cream. Makes 8 tartlets.

Strawberry-Rhubarb Petites

The quintessential summer fruit combination of strawberries and rhubarb has never tasted better than in these minimalist pastries.

1	pint strawberries, hulled and coarsely chopped
1¼	cups fresh or frozen (thawed) rhubarb, cut into ½-inch pieces
¾	cup sugar
1	teaspoon fresh lemon juice
2	tablespoons cornstarch
1	17.3-ounce package frozen puff pastry (2 sheets), thawed for 30 minutes
2	tablespoons powdered sugar

✳ In a saucepan combine strawberries, rhubarb, sugar, lemon juice, and cornstarch. Cook over medium-high heat 10 minutes. Reduce heat to medium; cook 2 minutes, until liquid is thickened, clear and bubbly. Let cool to room temperature.

✳ Preheat oven to 400°F.

✳ Unfold pastry sheets on lightly floured surface. Cut each sheet into 4 equal pieces. Coat 8 standard-size muffin cups with nonstick cooking spray. Gently press middle of 1 pastry square into bottom of muffin cup. Fill with almost ¼ cup of filling. For each cup, fold over the 4 corner pastry flaps, one on top of the other, covering the filling; brush with water to seal. Repeat with remaining puff pastry and filling.

✳ Bake 15–20 minutes, until tops are puffed and golden brown. Cool in pan on rack 10 minutes. Remove from muffin cups to rack; cool 5–10 minutes. Dust with powdered sugar. Makes 8 small pastries.

✳ *Cookies & Other Petite Confections*

Puff Pastry Cinnamon Rolls

Can cinnamon rolls be both traditional and surprising? Enlightened and simplified with puff pasty, the answer is an emphatic "yes!"

I	tablespoon butter
I	8-ounce package cream cheese, cubed
I	tablespoon ground cinnamon
I½	teaspoons vanilla extract
I	17.3-ounce package frozen puff pastry (2 sheets), thawed for 30 minutes
I	16-ounce container cream cheese frosting

✳ Line a baking sheet with parchment paper.

✳ In a saucepan melt butter over medium heat. Add cream cheese, cinnamon, and vanilla to pan, and stir until smooth. Remove from heat and cool for 10 minutes.

✳ Unfold 1 puff pastry sheet on a lightly floured work surface. Spread pastry with half of the cinnamon—cream cheese mixture. Roll puff pastry into a log. Repeat with remaining puff pastry sheet and filling. Refrigerate logs 30 minutes.

✳ Preheat oven to 375°F. Cut each log into 6 slices. Place slices on prepared sheet.

✳ Bake rolls 15–20 minutes or until puffed and golden brown. Remove from oven and spread cream cheese frosting over warm rolls. Serve warm or at room temperature. Makes 12 rolls.

Cookies & Other Petite Confections ✳

Italian Cream Tarts

The creamy custard filling in these classic Roman tarts has a mellow flavor with hints of orange. The mascarpone is a buttery-rich double cream hailing from the Lombardy region of Italy. If it is unavailable, an equal amount of cream cheese may be substituted.

⅓ cup sugar

¼ cup all-purpose flour

1 cup milk (not nonfat)

3 large egg yolks, lightly beaten

2 tablespoons orange liqueur

1 17.3-ounce package frozen puff pastry (2 sheets), thawed for 30 minutes

1 8-ounce container mascarpone cheese, room temperature

4 ounces semisweet chocolate, chopped

1 tablespoon vegetable shortening

3 cups assorted fresh berries (optional)

✳ Combine sugar and flour in a medium saucepan. Gradually whisk in milk. Whisk in egg yolks. Cook and stir over medium heat until thickened and bubbly. Remove from heat. Stir liqueur into pastry cream; pour into a bowl and cover surface with plastic wrap. Cool until lukewarm then chill until cold.

✳ Preheat oven to 400°F. Line 2 baking sheets with parchment paper.

✳ Unfold pastry sheets on a lightly floured surface. Roll out each pastry sheet to a 13-inch square.

✳ Using a 3-inch cookie cutter, cut out about 20 tarts (be sure to cut out an even number); place half of them on 1 of the prepared baking sheets and prick each a few times with a fork. Using a 2-inch cutter (of the same design or round), cut the middle out of the remaining pastries, reserving cutouts.

✳ Brush edges of the tarts on baking sheet with water and top with tarts that have the middles cut out. Press gently to fuse layers together to form taller tart shells. Arrange small cutouts on second baking sheet.

✳ Bake tart pastries 10–12 minutes, and cutouts 7–9 minutes. Cool pastries completely.

✳ Up to 1 hour before serving time, add mascarpone cheese to chilled pastry cream;

Cookies & Other Petite Confections

beat with an electric mixer on low speed until smooth. Carefully spoon mixture into tart shells.

❋ Melt semisweet chocolate and shortening together in a small saucepan over very low heat, stirring constantly. Remove from heat. Spread a thin layer of chocolate over tops of small cutouts. Pipe or drizzle remaining chocolate over the cream-filled tarts; refrigerate both until chocolate is set.

❋ To serve, arrange filled tarts and chocolate-glazed cutouts on large platter and surround with berries. Makes 20 tarts.

✔ **Cook's Note:** *The pastry cream may be made ahead of time. Cool, cover, and chill up to 4 hours before adding the cheese.*

Blueberry-Peach Pastry Hearts

Heart-shaped puff pastry cutouts showcase summer blueberries and peaches at their peak.

I	17.3-ounce package frozen puff pastry (2 sheets), thawed for 30 minutes
⅓	cup peach spreadable fruit or preserves
I	teaspoon finely shredded lemon zest
I	cup peeled and finely chopped fresh or frozen (thawed) peaches
I	cup fresh blueberries
I	8-ounce package cream cheese, softened
¼	cup packed brown sugar
I	teaspoon vanilla extract
2	tablespoons powdered sugar

✳ Preheat oven to 375°F. Line baking sheet with parchment paper.

✳ Unfold puff pastry sheets onto a lightly floured surface. Using a floured, 2-inch heart-shaped cookie cutter or a sharp small knife and a heart pattern, cut pastry into about 20 heart shapes (do not re-roll scraps). Place pastry hearts on prepared baking sheet.

✳ Bake 10–12 minutes or until puffed and golden. Cool on a wire rack.

✳ In a small saucepan combine spreadable fruit and lemon zest. Heat and stir until melted; cool. In a large mixing bowl combine peaches and blueberries. Add melted spreadable fruit mixture and gently toss to combine; set aside.

✳ In a medium mixing bowl beat cream cheese, brown sugar, and vanilla with an electric mixer on medium-high speed until fluffy.

✳ To assemble pastries, cut pastry hearts in half horizontally with a serrated knife. Spread each of the bottom halves with about I teaspoon cream cheese mixture. Top each with a spoonful of fruit mixture and a pastry top. Serve immediately or cover and chill for up to 4 hours. Just before serving, lightly sprinkle with powdered sugar. Makes about 20 pastries.

✔ **Cook's Note:** *The pastries may be made ahead of time. Bake pastry hearts. Cool and store tightly covered up to 12 hours ahead. Assemble pastries, cover, and chill for up to 4 hours ahead.*

Apple-Cherry Danish

Canned apple pie filling and dried cranberries are the secrets to these easy but impressive Danish.

1	21-ounce can apple-pie filling
⅓	cup dried tart cherries
1	tablespoon fresh lemon juice
1	17.3-ounce package frozen puff pastry (2 sheets), thawed for 30 minutes
1	large egg, beaten
2	teaspoons sugar

✴ Preheat oven to 400°F. Line a baking sheet with parchment paper.

✴ In a medium bowl mix apple pie filling, dried cherries, and lemon juice.

✴ On lightly floured surface roll out 1 of the pastry sheets to a 10-inch square. Place pastry square on one end of prepared baking sheet. Gently fold over 1 side of pastry so edge meets center; do not press fold. With small sharp knife, make 9 parallel cuts along folded edge, 1 inch apart and 2 inches deep. Unfold pastry.

✴ On other half of pastry (without the slits), spoon half of the apple mixture, leaving a ¾-inch border on 3 sides. Lightly brush edges of pastry with some water. Fold side of pastry with cuts over filling; press edges gently to seal. Repeat with second pastry sheet and remaining filling.

✴ Brush pastries with beaten egg; sprinkle with sugar.

✴ Bake 25–30 minutes until puffed and golden, covering edges with foil if they begin to get too brown. Cool slightly on wire rack to serve warm. Makes 16 servings.

Milk Chocolate Cashew Sachets

Tasting much like a gussied-up candy bar, these unabashedly rich treats derive their flavor and flair from a short list of readily available ingredients.

½ of a 17.3-ounce package frozen puff pastry (1 sheet), thawed for 30 minutes

2 milk chocolate candy bars, broken into segments

3 tablespoons light brown sugar

3 tablespoons finely chopped roasted, lightly salted cashews

2 teaspoons sugar

✳ Preheat oven to 400° F. Line baking sheet with parchment paper.

✳ Roll out pastry sheet on lightly floured surface to a 10x15-inch rectangle. Cut into twelve (12) 3x4-inch rectangles.

✳ In a microwave-safe bowl combine chocolate and brown sugar. Microwave on high power for 1½ minutes. Stir until melted (need not be completely melted). Stir in cashews.

✳ Spoon a heaping teaspoon of chocolate mixture in center of each pastry rectangle. Lightly brush the inside edges of each pastry rectangle with water. Fold the first flap three-quarters the way up to cover the filling; then fold the second flap approximately ¼ inch over the first fold. Press edges together firmly to seal; crimp side edges with a fork.

✳ Place on prepared baking sheet. Lightly brush with water and sprinkle with granulated sugar.

✳ Bake 12–14 minutes or until golden brown. Remove to wire rack. Serve warm or room temperature. Makes 12 pastries.

✔ **Cook's Note:** *To reheat, place in microwave on high power for 10–15 seconds.*

Toffee Turnovers

Toffee, cream cheese, pecans, and puff pastry? As you can likely imagine, these are incredibly delicious.

½ of a 17.3-ounce package frozen puff pastry (1 sheet), thawed for 30 minutes

2 3-ounce packages cream cheese, softened

2 tablespoons light brown sugar

½ teaspoon vanilla extract

3 milk chocolate-covered English toffee bars, chopped

1 cup chopped pecans, toasted

1 large egg, lightly beaten

✱ Preheat oven to 400°F. Line a baking sheet with parchment paper.

✱ Roll out pastry on lightly floured surface to a 14-inch square. Cut into 9 equal squares.

✱ In a medium bowl mix cream cheese, brown sugar, and vanilla with an electric mixer set on medium speed until well blended. Add toffee and pecans; mix well.

✱ Spoon filling evenly onto centers of pastry squares. Brush edges of pastry with egg. Fold each square diagonally in half to form triangle; press edges firmly together until completely sealed. Transfer pastries to prepared baking sheet and brush tops with remaining egg.

✱ Bake 10 minutes. Reduce oven temperature to 375°F. Continue baking 8–10 minutes longer or until turnovers are slightly puffed and golden brown. Cool 5 minutes before serving. Makes 9 turnovers.

Caramel Nut Napoleons

Sheer caramel heaven, these luscious pastries combine alternating layers of crisp pastry, gooey caramel, and crunchy nuts.

½ of a 17.3-ounce package frozen puff pastry (1 sheet), thawed for 30 minutes

¾ cup heavy whipping cream, well chilled

½ cup plus 2 tablespoons premium caramel ice cream topping, divided use

½ cup chopped toasted pecans

2 tablespoons powdered sugar

✳ Preheat oven to 400°F. Line a baking sheet with parchment paper.

✳ Unfold pastry sheet on lightly floured surface. Cut into 3 lengthwise strips along fold marks. Cut each strip crosswise into 3 squares; place on prepared baking sheet.

✳ Bake 12–15 minutes or until golden brown. Remove to wire racks and cool completely.

✳ In a medium bowl whip the cream and 2 tablespoons of the caramel topping with an electric mixer until stiff peaks form. Loosely cover and refrigerate until ready to use.

✳ Split each pastry square horizontally into 2 layers, making a total of 18 squares. Set aside the 9 top layers. Spoon 3 tablespoons of the caramel cream onto each bottom layer. Drizzle evenly with some of the remaining ½ cup caramel topping and sprinkle with pecans. Cover with pastry tops and sprinkle with powdered sugar. Serve right away. Store leftover desserts in refrigerator. Makes 9 napoleons.

Berry Napoleons with Lavender Honey Cream

These easy-to-make napoleons raise the elegance quotient with a vibrant mix of fresh berries and silky lavender honey-mascarpone filling.

½	of a 17.3-ounce package frozen puff pastry (1 sheet), thawed for 30 minutes
1	large egg
1	tablespoon whole milk
1	tablespoon sugar
1	cup heavy whipping cream
1	8-ounce container mascarpone cheese, room temperature
¼	cup lavender honey
1	cup sliced fresh strawberries
½	cup fresh raspberries
½	cup fresh blueberries
2	tablespoons fresh orange juice
¼	cup powdered sugar

✳ Preheat oven to 375°F. Line a baking sheet with parchment paper.

✳ Roll pastry out on a lightly floured work surface to a 9 x 12-inch rectangle. Cut eight (8) 3x4½-inch rectangles from puff pastry and arrange about 1 inch apart on prepared baking sheet.

✳ In a small bowl beat egg with milk until blended. Brush tops of rectangles lightly with egg wash, and sprinkle with sugar.

✳ Bake 20–25 minutes until golden brown, rotating sheet after 10 minutes to ensure even baking. Remove from oven and cool on wire racks.

✳ In bowl of an electric mixer, beat cream, mascarpone, and honey on medium-high speed until thickened, about 5 minutes. In a small bowl combine strawberries, raspberries, and blueberries. Add orange juice and powdered sugar and toss to coat. Let rest for at least 15 minutes.

✳ To assemble, use a serrated knife to carefully slice each rectangle into thirds horizontally. Place bottom third on a serving plate, and add a spoonful of berries. Spoon a scant ¼ cup of cream mixture over berries and cover with middle section. Repeat with berries and cream. Place last third of pastry on top. Repeat with remaining ingredients and serve. Makes 8 napoleons.

Cookies & Other Petite Confections

Grand Desserts

Quick Apple Tart

Easy enough to make on weeknights but elegant enough to serve at a dinner party, this tart is a home baker's dream come true. It is equally delicious made with fresh sliced peaches, pears, or nectarines.

½ of a 17.3-ounce package frozen puff pastry (1 sheet), thawed for 30 minutes

3 medium Golden Delicious apples, peeled, cored, very thinly sliced

2 tablespoons (¼ stick) unsalted butter, melted

3 tablespoons sugar

½ teaspoon ground cinnamon

¼ cup apple jelly

✳ Preheat oven to 400°F. Line a baking sheet with parchment paper.

✳ Unfold pastry on prepared baking sheet. Using tines of fork, pierce ½-inch border around edge of pastry, then pierce center all over.

✳ Arrange apples atop pastry in 4 rows, overlapping apple slices and leaving the ½-inch border uncovered. Brush apples with melted butter. Combine sugar and cinnamon in a small cup; sprinkle over apples.

✳ Bake 25–28 minutes until golden. Melt the jelly in a small saucepan set over low heat. Brush melted jelly over apples. Bake tart 5 minutes longer. Serve warm or at room temperature. Makes 6 servings.

Orange Cream Tart with Pistachios

A combination of very common ingredients—canned mandarin oranges, a block of cream cheese, a package of frozen puff pastry, and pre-shelled pistachios—is the secret to this elegant, yet easy, tart.

½ of a 17.3-ounce package frozen puff pastry (1 sheet), thawed for 30 minutes

1 large egg, lightly beaten

2 tablespoons sugar

1 navel orange

3 10-ounce cans mandarin oranges, drained

1 8-ounce package cream cheese, softened

¼ cup powdered sugar

½ teaspoon vanilla

2 tablespoons shelled salted roasted pistachios (not dyed red), chopped

✳ Preheat oven to 425°F. Line a baking sheet with parchment paper.

✳ Unfold pastry sheet on a lightly floured surface and roll out to a 12-inch square. Trim a ¾-inch-wide strip from all sides of square and reserve.

✳ Put pastry square on prepared baking sheet and prick all over with a fork. Brush pastry square with some of egg and arrange 1 strip on each edge of pastry square, overlapping strips at corners, to form a raised edge around pastry. Trim overhang. Brush strips with some of egg, then sprinkle pastry evenly with sugar.

✳ Bake in middle of oven until golden brown, 15–17 minutes. Carefully slide pastry from baking sheet to a rack to cool. Gently flatten inner part of pastry with palm or spatula if very puffed. Cool.

✳ Grate 1 teaspoon zest from the navel orange. Squeeze 2 tablespoons juice from the same navel orange. Arrange mandarin orange slices in 1 layer between paper towels to drain briefly.

✳ In a medium bowl beat together cream cheese, powdered sugar, vanilla, orange zest, and orange juice with an electric mixer set on medium speed until blended and smooth. Spread evenly over center of pastry, spreading it to raised border.

✳ Arrange mandarin oranges, overlapping, on pastry and sprinkle with pistachios. Makes 6 servings.

Grand Desserts

Warm Chocolate Banana-Nut Tarts

Melted chocolate, sweet, warm bananas, and a creamy, nutty filling? Skip dinner and start with dessert.

⅔	cup packed light brown sugar
6	tablespoons (¾ stick) unsalted butter, softened
2	large egg yolks
2	tablespoons all purpose flour
⅔	cup finely chopped lightly salted roasted peanuts
1	17.3-ounce package frozen puff pastry (2 sheets), thawed
1	large egg, lightly beaten
4	medium bananas, peeled, thinly sliced into rounds
1	cup miniature semisweet chocolate chips

✳ Preheat oven to 350°F. Line 2 baking sheets with parchment paper.

✳ Using electric mixer, beat brown sugar and butter in medium bowl until well blended. Beat in yolks. Mix in flour, then peanuts. Set peanut cream aside.

✳ Unfold pastry sheets on a lightly floured surface. Cut each pastry sheet into 4 squares and pierce all over with fork. Place 4 pastry squares on each of 2 baking sheets, spacing apart. Lightly brush egg over pastry.

✳ Spread 2 tablespoons peanut cream over each pastry, leaving ½-inch plain border. Arrange bananas in overlapping slices atop peanut cream. Sprinkle each pastry with 2 tablespoons miniature chocolate chips.

✳ Bake until crusts are golden brown, about 25–28 minutes. Transfer to plates. Serve warm. Makes 8 servings.

Rhubarb-Ricotta Tart

The contrast of cool creamy ricotta with tart-sweet rhubarb filling sings summer. But you can actually make this tart year-round—just look for bags of frozen, cut rhubarb in the freezer section of the grocery store where frozen fruit is stored.

I pound rhubarb, sliced ½-inch thick

1¼ cups plus 1½ tablespoons packed light brown sugar, divided use

½ of a 17.3-ounce package frozen puff pastry (I sheet), thawed for 30 minutes

I cup whole-milk ricotta cheese

⅓ cup powdered sugar

I large egg, lightly beaten

✳ Combine rhubarb and 1¼ cups brown sugar in a large saucepan. Cook over low heat until syrup forms and rhubarb is tender but not falling apart, stirring occasionally, about 35 minutes. Pour rhubarb mixture into colander set over a large bowl. Cover colander and chill rhubarb and juices overnight.

✳ Preheat oven to 400°F. Line a baking sheet with parchment paper.

✳ Roll out pastry sheet on floured surface to a 12-inch square. Place pastry on prepared baking sheet and pierce all over with fork. Bake 5 minutes. Remove from oven and flatten with spatula.

✳ Return pastry to oven and bake until golden, about 10 minutes longer.

✳ Blend ricotta and powdered sugar in a small bowl. Brush pastry with beaten egg. Leaving ½-inch plain border, spread cheese mixture over pastry. Bake about 10 minutes. Remove to a cooling rack.

✳ Preheat broiler. Pour rhubarb juices into small saucepan. Boil until reduced to thick syrup, stirring occasionally, about 8 minutes. Spread rhubarb ¾-inch-thick on rimmed baking sheet. Sprinkle with remaining 1½ tablespoons brown sugar. Broil until top is crisp and dark brown in spots, about 4 minutes.

✳ Spoon the broiled rhubarb over tart. Cut into 4 pieces, drizzle with rhubarb syrup, and serve. Makes 4 servings.

Grand Desserts

Mango Margarita Tart

This tart delivers fresh flavors in a flash that are reminiscent of a margarita—perfect for a south-of-the-border grill party or any other summer meal.

½	of a 17.3-ounce package frozen puff pastry (1 sheet), thawed for 30 minutes
1	large egg, lightly beaten
4	tablespoons sugar, divided use
½	cup sour cream
⅔	cup whipped cream cheese
1	tablespoon fresh lime juice
1½	teaspoons grated lime zest
2	large firm-ripe mangoes, peeled
¼	cup apple jelly
	Fresh mint leaves (optional)

✳ Preheat oven to 400°F. Line a baking sheet with parchment paper.

✳ Unfold pastry sheet on a prepared baking sheet, then turn over (to prevent creases from splitting during baking). Trim edges with a sharp knife. Brush pastry lightly with egg (do not allow to drip down sides). Create a ¾-inch border all around by lightly scoring a line parallel to each edge of pastry (do not cut all the way through). Prick inner rectangle evenly with a fork, then sprinkle with 1 tablespoon sugar.

✳ Bake in lower third of oven 15 minutes or until puffed and golden brown. Transfer to a rack and cool to room temperature.

✳ In a small bowl whisk the sour cream, cream cheese, lime juice, lime zest and remaining 3 tablespoons sugar until blended.

✳ Thinly slice mangoes lengthwise with a mandoline or a sharp knife then halve wide slices lengthwise.

✳ Just before serving, spread cream over inner rectangle of pastry and top with mangoes, overlapping decoratively. Melt the jelly in a small saucepan set over low heat. Brush melted jelly over mangoes. If desired, garnish with fresh mint leaves. Makes 8 servings.

Grand Desserts ✳

Festive, delicious, and relaxed—just what a company-worthy dessert should be, and exactly what this blueberry tart is.

½ of a 17.3-ounce package frozen puff pastry (1 sheet), thawed for 30 minutes
1 large egg, lightly beaten
2 tablespoons sugar
1 8-ounce package cream cheese, softened
2 tablespoons half and half
3 tablespoons powdered sugar
¾ teaspoon almond extract
¼ cup red currant jelly
2 teaspoons lemon juice
2½ cups fresh blueberries
½ cup sliced almonds, lightly toasted (optional)

✳ Preheat oven to 425°F. Line a baking sheet with parchment paper.

✳ Unfold pastry sheet on a lightly floured surface and roll out to a 12-inch square. Brush off excess flour from top and bottom of square and from work surface. Trim a ¾-inch-wide strip from all sides of square and reserve.

✳ Put pastry square on prepared baking sheet and prick all over with a fork. Brush pastry square with some of egg and arrange 1 strip on each edge of pastry square, overlapping strips at corners, to form a raised edge around pastry, and trim overhang. Brush strips with some of egg. Sprinkle pastry evenly with sugar.

✳ Bake in middle of oven 15–17 minutes until golden brown. Carefully slide pastry from baking sheet (using parchment paper) to a rack to cool, then gently flatten inner part of pastry with palm or spatula if very puffed. Cool.

✳ In a small bowl whisk together cream cheese, half and half, powdered sugar, and almond extract until blended and smooth. Spread evenly over center of pastry, spreading it to raised edges.

✳ In a small saucepan set over medium heat bring jelly to a boil with lemon juice, whisking until smooth. Toss glaze with blueberries in a medium bowl and spoon blueberries onto tart to cover cream. If desired, garnish with toasted almonds. Makes 6 servings.

Grand Desserts

Fresh Nectarine Tart with Sour Cream Topping

Here's a summer-fresh tart that will bring bright taste and casual sophistication to your next outdoor get-together. Don't bother removing the skin from the nectarines—not only is it very thin and edible, it also adds beautiful shades of gold and red to the tart.

½   of a 17.3-ounce package frozen puff pastry (1 sheet), thawed for 30 minutes

1   large egg, lightly beaten

½   cup chopped pecans, toasted

7   tablespoons sugar, divided use

2   tablespoons all-purpose flour

1¾ pounds nectarines (about 5 or 6 large), pitted, cut into ⅓-inch-thick wedges

⅓   cup peach or apricot preserves

1   tablespoon water

½   cup chilled heavy whipping cream

¼   cup sour cream

✳ Position rack in bottom third of oven and preheat to 400°F. Line a baking sheet with parchment paper.

✳ Roll out puff pastry on lightly floured work surface into a 14-inch square. Cut off 1-inch-wide strips from each side of square. Brush strips with beaten egg. Place strips atop edges of pastry square, egg side down, pressing to adhere. Trim ends to fit.

✳ Transfer pastry square to prepared baking sheet. In a small bowl combine pecans, 2 tablespoons sugar, and flour. Sprinkle evenly over bottom of pastry.

✳ Place nectarines in large bowl. Add 4 tablespoons of the remaining sugar; toss to coat. Arrange nectarines decoratively over pecan mixture.

✳ Bake tart until pastry is golden brown and puffed and nectarines are tender, about 30 minutes. Transfer pan to rack. Using parchment paper, transfer tart to cooling rack, leaving tart on parchment.

✳ In a small heavy saucepan stir preserves and water over low heat until preserves melt. Brush over warm nectarines.

✳ Beat cream, sour cream, and remaining 1 tablespoon sugar in medium bowl with electric mixer set on high speed until soft peaks form. Serve tart warm or at room temperature with sour cream topping. Makes 6 servings.

Grand Desserts

Tropical Fruit Tart with Rum Filling

Complete the island-inspired theme here by pairing this gorgeous fruit tart with ice-cold tropical drinks garnished with paper umbrellas.

½	of a 17.3-ounce package frozen puff pastry (1 sheet), thawed for 30 minutes
1	8-ounce package cream cheese, softened
⅓	cup powdered sugar
2	tablespoons dark rum
1	teaspoon grated lime zest
3	kiwifruit, peeled, halved lengthwise, and cut into thin slices
1	firm-ripe mango, peeled, pitted, and cut into thin slices
1	cup fresh raspberries
3	tablespoons apple jelly

✳ Preheat oven to 400°F. Line a baking sheet with parchment paper.

✳ Unfold pastry on lightly floured surface and roll out to a 14 x 10-inch rectangle. Place pastry on prepared baking sheet and brush edges with water. Fold over ½ inch around all sides and press firmly into bottom of pastry to form rim. Pierce pastry all over inside of rim with a fork.

✳ Bake 14–17 minutes or until golden brown, breaking any large air bubbles with fork after the first 10 minutes. Cool completely on wire rack.

✳ In a medium bowl beat cream cheese, powered sugar, rum, and lime zest with electric mixer set on medium speed until well blended. Spread onto cooled pastry.

✳ Arrange kiwi, mango, and raspberries over cream filling. Melt jelly in a small saucepan set over low heat. Brush melted jelly over fruit just before serving. Makes 4–6 servings.

✳ *Grand Desserts*

Swiss Honey-Almond Tart

Calling all home bakers: this humble list of everyday ingredients bakes up into a supremely delicious European-style confection in no time.

$\frac{1}{3}$ cup plus 1 tablespoon whipping cream, divided use

$\frac{1}{4}$ cup honey

1 tablespoon unsalted butter

$\frac{2}{3}$ cup sugar

3 tablespoons water

1 tablespoon fresh lemon juice

$\frac{1}{2}$ teaspoon almond extract

1 17.3-ounce package frozen puff pastry (2 sheets), thawed for 30 minutes

2 cups coarsely chopped almonds

1 large egg, beaten to blend

1 large egg yolk

✳ In a small saucepan over medium heat stir $\frac{1}{3}$ cup cream, honey, and butter until butter melts. Set aside.

✳ In a medium-size heavy saucepan over low heat stir sugar, water, and lemon juice until sugar dissolves. Increase heat; boil without stirring until syrup turns golden, occasionally swirling pan and brushing down sides with wet pastry brush, about 12 minutes. Remove from heat. Add warm cream mixture (mixture will bubble up). Stir over very low heat until smooth. Add almond extract. Transfer to bowl and chill uncovered until cold, about 1 hour.

✳ Roll out 1 pastry sheet on lightly floured surface into 11-inch square. Using 10-inch-diameter cake pan bottom as guide, trim to 10-inch round. Transfer to a baking sheet lined with parchment paper. Roll out second pastry sheet to an 11-inch square. Using 11-inch-diameter tart pan bottom as guide, trim to 11-inch round. Using fork, pierce the 11-inch round; cut out small hole from center.

✳ Mix almonds into cold caramel mixture. Brush beaten egg in 1-inch border on the pastry on baking sheet. Spread almond-caramel mixture over pastry, mounding in center and leaving 1-inch border. Cover with 11-inch round. Press to seal. Fold edge of bottom pastry over top pastry. Seal edge tightly. Mix remaining 1 tablespoon cream and yolk into remaining beaten egg. Brush top of tart with egg mixture. Chill tart on baking sheet 1 hour.

✳ Preheat oven to 400°F. Bake tart until golden, about 25 minutes. Cool. Makes 8 servings.

Grand Desserts ✳

Italian Fresh Grape Tart

If you think fresh grapes are just for snacking, think again. They also make a variety of stylish desserts, including this Italian-inspired fruit tart. Not only is it sophisticated, simple to prepare, and delicious, it is also very economical.

$5\frac{1}{2}$ cups red and green seedless grapes (about $2\frac{1}{4}$ pounds)

$\frac{1}{4}$ cup sugar

4 tablespoons all purpose flour, divided use

1 teaspoon fresh lemon juice

$\frac{1}{2}$ of a 17.3-ounce package frozen puff pastry (1 sheet), thawed for 30 minutes

1 tablespoon unsalted butter

✳ Purée $\frac{3}{4}$ cup grapes in processor. Strain grape purée, pressing on solids to extract as much juice as possible. Pour $\frac{1}{4}$ cup grape juice into large bowl; discard any remaining juice. Cut $2\frac{1}{2}$ cups grapes lengthwise in half; add cut grapes and remaining whole grapes to juice in bowl. Add sugar, 3 tablespoons flour, and lemon juice; toss to blend well. Let stand 30 minutes, stirring occasionally.

✳ Preheat oven to 375°F. Line a baking sheet with parchment paper.

✳ Roll out pastry sheet on a lightly floured surface to an 11-inch square. Transfer pastry to prepared baking sheet.

✳ Sprinkle remaining 1 tablespoon flour over center of pastry, leaving $2\frac{1}{2}$-inch plain border. Spoon grape mixture, including juices, into center of pastry. Fold pastry edges up over grapes, forming 2- to $2\frac{1}{2}$-inch border. Dot grapes with 1 tablespoon butter.

✳ **Bake tart until crust is golden brown and grape juices are bubbling, about 45 minutes (crust border will unfold slightly). Cool tart to room temperature. Makes 6 servings.**

Grand Desserts

Apricot, Honey & Goat Cheese Tarts

Goat cheese and fruit? Absolutely—it's a heavenly match. This uncomplicated, elegant dessert makes a fresh finale to dinner on a hot summer day.

I	large egg yolk
I	teaspoon water
I	17.3-ounce package frozen puff pastry (2 sheets), thawed for 30 minutes
3	tablespoons sugar
2	4-ounce packages goat cheese, softened
4	tablespoons honey, divided use
I	tablespoon grated lemon zest
2	pounds fresh apricots, pitted and quartered
¼	cup snipped fresh mint

✳ Preheat oven to 425°F. Line 2 baking sheets with parchment paper.

✳ In a small bowl mix egg yolk with water. Set aside.

✳ Unfold the pastry sheets on a lightly floured surface. Roll gently to flatten creases forming two 10-inch squares. Cut ½-inch strips from all 4 sides of each pastry sheet. Brush the edges of the pastry sheets with the egg mixture. Place the cut strips on top and along edges of the pastry sheets, gently pressing in place to form a raised edge; trim any overlaps.

✳ Place pastries on prepared baking sheets. Brush pastries with egg mixture. Prick pastry with a fork. Sprinkle with sugar. Bake, 1 sheet at a time, 17–20 minutes or until puffed and golden brown. Refrigerate second sheet while baking first. Cool on baking sheets on wire racks.

✳ In a small bowl stir together goat cheese, 2 tablespoons honey, and the lemon zest. Spread over bottom of tart shells.

✳ Arrange apricot quarters on top of the goat cheese mixture, overlapping slightly. Drizzle with remaining 2 tablespoons honey. Sprinkle with fresh mint. Slide onto cutting board or serving platter and cut each tart into quarters. Makes 8 servings.

✔ **Cook's Note:** *Tart shells may also be baked up to 4 hours ahead; cover and store at room temperature. Assemble tarts just before serving.*

Grand Desserts ✳

Almond Cream "King's Cake" Tart
(Galette de Rois)

"King's Cake" is the traditional cake served during Twelfth Night. It comes in all sorts of shapes and sizes, but it always has a bean or other token baked inside. The recipient of the piece of cake with the bean inside is supposed to have guaranteed good luck.

¼	cup pure almond paste
¼	cup granulated sugar
3	tablespoons unsalted butter, softened
2	large eggs, divided use
¼	teaspoon vanilla
¼	teaspoon almond extract
2	tablespoons all-purpose flour
I	17.3-ounce package frozen puff pastry (2 sheets), thawed for 30 minutes
I	dried bean such as a lima bean (optional)
½	tablespoon powdered sugar

✳ Preheat oven to 450°F. Line a baking sheet with parchment paper.

✳ Purée almond paste, granulated sugar, butter, and a pinch of salt in a food processor until smooth. Add I of the eggs, vanilla, and almond extract. Process until blended. Add flour and pulse until incorporated.

✳ On a lightly floured surface roll out I puff pastry sheet into an 11½-inch square. Brush off excess flour from both sides. Cut out an 11-inch round by tracing around an inverted plate with tip of a paring knife. Transfer round to prepared baking sheet. Chill. Repeat procedure with second pastry sheet, leaving round on floured surface.

✳ Beat remaining egg with a fork and brush some over top of second round. Score round decoratively all over using tip of knife, then make several small slits all the way through pastry, at about 2-inch intervals, to create steam vents.

✳ Brush some of egg in a I-inch-wide border around edge of chilled pastry round (on baking sheet). Mound almond cream in center of chilled round, spreading slightly, and bury bean in cream. Immediately cover with decorated round and press edges together lightly. Holding a small spoon with side at an angle, press around edge to seal tart decoratively.

Grand Desserts

Bake tart in lower third of oven until puffed and pale golden, 13–15 minutes. Sprinkle tart with powdered sugar and bake in upper third of oven until edge is deep golden brown and shiny, 12–15 minutes more. Transfer to a rack to cool slightly, 5–10 minutes. Serve warm. Makes 8 servings.

Grand Desserts

French Fruit Tart

So simple to prepare, the key to this versatile tart is to use the best fruit of the season. So use this as a template and let the bounty of the market, and your imagination, be your guide.

½   of a 17.3-ounce package frozen puff pastry (1 sheet), thawed for 30 minutes

1   3-ounce package cream cheese, softened

¼   cup heavy whipping cream

2   tablespoons sugar

1   tablespoon plus 1 teaspoon orange-flavor liqueur, divided use

4   ounces seedless red grapes (about ¾ cup), each cut in half

2   ripe kiwifruit, peeled, each cut lengthwise in half, then thinly sliced crosswise

½   pint medium strawberries (about 1½ cups), hulled, each cut lengthwise in half

2   tablespoons apricot jam, melted

✳ Preheat oven to 400°F. Line a baking sheet with parchment paper.

✳ On lightly floured surface, unfold puff pastry sheet. Cut pastry along a fold line to remove 1 strip (about 9 x 3 inches); set aside. Roll remaining larger pastry piece into a 14x8-inch rectangle. Transfer to prepared baking sheet. With sharp knife, trim pastry to make straight edges.

✳ On lightly floured surface roll the reserved pastry strip into a 16x3-inch rectangle; fold in half to form an 8x3-inch rectangle, then cut lengthwise into 3 equal strips. Unfold strips.

✳ Moisten edges of pastry on cookie sheet with finger dipped in water. Place 1 pastry strip on dampened edge of each long side of rectangle; trim to fit. Cut remaining pastry strip crosswise in half and place each half along short sides of rectangle, over-lapping strips on long sides. Lightly roll over dough with rolling pin to seal edges. With fork, prick dough rectangle (inside of strips) at ¼-inch intervals to prevent puffing during baking.

✳ Bake tart shell 13–15 minutes or until lightly browned. (If center of pastry puffs up, open oven and press down with spatula after 7 minutes baking.) Using parchment paper remove pastry from baking sheet. Cool on wire rack.

✳ Meanwhile, in small bowl whisk cream cheese, heavy cream, sugar, and 1 tablespoon liqueur until smooth.

Grand Desserts

❋ Spread cream-cheese filling into cooled pastry shell. Arrange a row of grape halves on filling down 1 long side of tart, then a row of kiwifruit slices, then a row of strawberry halves. Repeat rows with remaining fruit (you may have a few pieces of fruit left over).

❋ Stir remaining 1 teaspoon liqueur into apricot jam. Brush jam mixture over fruit. If not serving tart right away, cover and refrigerate up to 8 hours. Makes 6 servings.

Caramel Banana Upside-Down Tart

The mere thought of this caramelicious banana tart makes my mouth water (vanilla ice cream is a must-have accompaniment!). The tart is best eaten the day it's made, fresh from the oven or at room temperature—it shouldn't be a problem!

½ of a 17.3-ounce package frozen puff pastry (1 sheet), thawed for 30 minutes
2 tablespoons butter
½ cup jarred premium caramel ice cream topping
3 large bananas, peeled and thickly sliced
   Vanilla ice cream (optional)

✳ On a lightly floured surface roll the pastry out to a 10-inch square. Using a cake pan or plate as a guide, cut a 10-inch circle of dough from it. Prick all over with a fork. Loosely cover with plastic wrap and chill.

✳ Preheat oven to 425°F.

✳ Place a heavy 9- or 10-inch metal cake pan on the stove on a large burner and turn the heat onto medium. Add the butter and warm to melt it. Add the caramel and bring to a low boil, stirring a bit. Remove the pan from the heat and place the banana slices in the pan decoratively in concentric circles to cover the whole bottom of the pan.

✳ Unfold the pastry and place it over the bananas to cover them, tucking the pastry down along the inside of the pan (the pastry will shrink to fit the pan as it bakes).

✳ Bake 20–25 minutes until the pastry is golden brown. Let cool in the pan on a wire rack 30 minutes then warm the bottom of the pan on the stove for a minute and turn the tart out onto a serving platter. If desired, serve with vanilla ice cream. Makes 6–8 servings.

✳ *Grand Desserts*

Kiwi Cream Tart

Lively, springy, zingy—that's this tart.

- ½ of a 17.3-ounce package frozen puff pastry (1 sheet), thawed for 30 minutes
- 1 8-ounce package cream cheese, softened
- 2 tablespoons sugar
- 2 tablespoons fresh lime juice
- 1½ teaspoons grated lime zest
- 8 kiwis, peeled and sliced lengthwise
- ⅓ cup apple jelly

  Fresh mint leaves for garnish (optional)

✳ Preheat oven to 400°F. Line a baking sheet with parchment paper.

✳ Unfold pastry on lightly floured surface and roll out to a 14 x 10-inch rectangle. Place on prepared baking sheet. Brush edges of rectangle with water. Fold over ½ inch on all sides and press firmly to form rim. Prick pastry all over (inside rim) with fork.

✳ Bake 13–16 minutes or until golden. Transfer to a wire rack and cool completely.

✳ In a medium bowl mix the cream cheese, sugar, lime juice, and lime zest with an electric mixer set on medium speed until blended and smooth. Spread mixture evenly over pastry. Arrange kiwi in concentric circles to cover.

✳ Melt the jelly in a small saucepan set over low heat. Brush jelly over kiwi and, if desired, garnish with mint leaves. Serve immediately or chill up to 2 hours. Makes 6–8 servings.

Fresh Blackberry Tart with Mint Cream

Both fresh mint and blackberries sing summer. Together, they create perfect harmony.

½   of a 17.3-ounce package frozen puff pastry (2 sheets), thawed for 30 minutes

1   egg, lightly beaten with fork

½   cup whipping cream

1   3-ounce package cream cheese, softened and cut into small pieces

¼   cup powdered sugar

2   tablespoons snipped fresh mint

2   cups fresh blackberries

1–2   tablespoons powdered sugar

     Fresh mint sprigs for garnish

✳ Preheat oven to 400°F. Line a baking sheet with parchment paper.

✳ Unfold pastry sheet and cut a ¾-inch-wide strip off each side of the pastry and reserve. Roll out the pastry sheet on a lightly floured work surface to a 10-inch square. Place the square on prepared baking sheet. Brush the edges of the square with the egg. Working with 1 strip at a time, stand the strips along the edges of the pastry square and crimp where they meet. Overlap the strips at the corners.

✳ Brush the border with the beaten egg. Pierce the center of the pastry all over with fork. Bake until the pastry is golden brown, about 18–20 minutes. Transfer to a rack and cool completely.

✳ Just before serving, beat the cream in a medium bowl with an electric mixer until soft peaks form. With the mixer still running, gradually add the cream cheese and ¼ cup powdered sugar and continue to beat until blended. Stir in the snipped mint.

✳ Spoon the cream mixture into the prepared pastry crust. Arrange the berries over the cream. Sift with remaining 1–2 tablespoons powdered sugar, garnish with mint sprigs, and serve immediately. Makes 6 servings.

✔ **Cook's Note:** *The pastry shell may be made several hours ahead of time and filled with the cream and fruit just before serving.*

✳ *Grand Desserts*

Apple Tarte Tatin

Beloved by the French, tarte tatin—essentially an upside-down apple tart—perfumes the air with caramel and fresh apples as it bakes.

½   of a 17.3-ounce package frozen puff pastry (1 sheet), thawed for 30 minutes

½   stick (¼ cup) unsalted butter, softened

½   cup sugar

7–9   Gala apples (3–4 pounds total), peeled, quartered lengthwise, and cored

✳ Preheat oven to 425°F. Line a baking sheet with parchment paper.

✳ Roll out pastry sheet on a lightly floured work surface to a 10½-inch square. Brush off excess flour. Using a plate or cake pan as a guide, cut out a 10-inch round with a sharp knife. Transfer round to prepared baking sheet and chill.

✳ Spread butter thickly on bottom and side of a 10-inch, well-seasoned cast iron skillet and pour sugar evenly over bottom. Arrange as many apples as will fit vertically on sugar, packing them tightly in concentric circles (apples will stick up above rim of skillet.)

✳ Cook apples over moderately high heat, undisturbed, until juices are deep golden and bubbling, about 18–25 minutes.

✳ Put skillet in middle of oven over a piece of foil to catch any drips. Bake 20 minutes (apples will settle slightly), then remove from oven and lay pastry round over apples.

✳ Bake tart until pastry is golden brown, about 20–25 minutes. Transfer skillet to a rack and cool at least 10 minutes.

✳ Just before serving, invert a platter with lip over skillet and, using potholders to hold skillet and plate tightly together, invert tart onto platter. Replace any apples that stick to skillet. Makes 6 servings.

Grand Desserts ✳

Peach Tarte Tatin

At once simple and sublime, this fresh peach tart will provide the closing centerpiece for an evening of conversation and camaraderie.

⅔   cup premium jarred caramel ice cream topping

1   teaspoon fresh lemon juice

2   teaspoons grated lemon zest

5   medium unpeeled peaches, quartered, pitted

½   of a 17.3-ounce package frozen puff pastry (1 sheet), thawed for 30 minutes
     Sweetened whipped cream

✻ Preheat oven to 375°F. In a small bowl mix the caramel topping, lemon juice, and lemon zest. Spread caramel into nonstick 9-inch-diameter cake pan with 1½-inch-high sides.

✻ Place unpeeled peach quarters, skin-side down, in concentric circles atop caramel in cake pan, covering caramel completely. Bake until peaches are just tender, about 30 minutes. Remove cake pan from oven.

✻ Roll out puff pastry sheet on lightly floured work surface to a 10½-inch square. Using 10-inch-diameter tart pan bottom or plate as guide, cut out round. Pierce pastry all over with fork. Cover peaches in cake pan with pastry round. Press pastry down around peaches at edge of cake pan.

✻ Bake tart until pastry is puffed and deep golden, about 25–27 minutes. Let tart rest 5 minutes.

✻ Cut around edge of cake pan to loosen pastry. Place large platter over cake pan. Hold cake pan and platter firmly together and invert, allowing tart to settle onto platter. Carefully lift off cake pan. Rearrange any peaches that may have become dislodged. Cool tart 30 minutes. Cut warm tart into wedges; serve with whipped cream. Makes 6–8 servings.

✻ *Grand Desserts*

PEACH TARTE TATIN

Although this tarte tatin is a bit more time-consuming to prepare, it really is worth the effort. The peppery ginger gets mellow in the homemade caramel topping, and the vanilla brings out the perfume of the fresh pears.

½	of a 17.3-ounce package frozen puff pastry (1 sheet), thawed for 30 minutes
½	cup sugar
¼	cup water
1	teaspoon light corn syrup
2	tablespoons (¼ stick) unsalted butter
1	teaspoon vanilla extract
1	tablespoon grated, peeled fresh ginger
5	medium-size firm Anjou pears (about 2¼ pounds), peeled, halved, cored, each half cut into 4 wedges
	Whipped cream

✳ Roll out pastry on lightly floured surface to 10-inch square. Trim edges, making 10-inch-diameter round; pierce round all over with fork. Slide onto rimless baking sheet lined with parchment paper. Cover and chill pastry while preparing pears.

✳ Fill large skillet with ice and water; set aside. In a seasoned 10-inch cast iron skillet, stir the sugar, ¼ cup water, and corn syrup over low heat until sugar dissolves. Increase heat and boil until syrup is dark amber color, occasionally swirling and brushing down sides of skillet with wet pastry brush, about 5 minutes. Remove from heat; whisk in butter, then vanilla and ginger (caramel will bubble up).

✳ Arrange pears, cut-side down and overlapping, in circle in skillet, placing a few around edge, if necessary. Place skillet over medium heat. Cook until pears are tender and syrup thickens enough to coat spoon, about 23 minutes. Place hot skillet atop ice in large skillet to cool pear mixture quickly. (Can be made 4 hours ahead. Let stand at room temperature.)

✳ Preheat oven to 375°F. Place puff pastry round atop pear mixture in skillet; tuck in edges around pears. Bake tart until pastry is puffed and golden, about 35 minutes. Cool tart completely in pan at least 1 hour and up to 6 hours.

✳ Preheat oven to 375°F. Re-warm tart in oven 8 minutes. Place platter atop skillet. Using oven mitts, hold skillet and platter together and turn over, releasing tart. Serve tart with whipped cream. Makes 6–8 servings.

Grand Desserts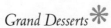

Banana Puffed Pie with Chocolate Rum Sauce

Bananas plus chocolate plus rum equals pure comfort food. Requests for seconds are imminent.

2	tablespoons (¼ stick) unsalted butter
⅓	cup sugar
3	tablespoons dark rum, divided use
1	tablespoon water
¼	teaspoon ground cinnamon
1¾	pounds ripe small bananas (about 5), peeled, left whole
6	ounces bittersweet (not unsweetened) or semisweet chocolate, chopped
¼	cup whipping cream
2	tablespoons light corn syrup
1	17.3-ounce package frozen puff pastry (2 sheets), thawed for 30 minutes
1	large egg, beaten to blend (glaze)

✳ In a large heavy skillet melt butter over medium heat. Add sugar, 1 tablespoon rum, water, and cinnamon and stir until syrupy. Add bananas and cook 2 minutes, turning occasionally and basting with syrup. Using slotted spoon, transfer bananas to plate. Boil syrup until reduced to 2 tablespoons, about 2 minutes. Pour syrup over bananas; let cool.

✳ In a small heavy saucepan combine chocolate, cream, and corn syrup; stir over low heat until chocolate melts and mixture is smooth. Remove from heat. Transfer 2 tablespoons chocolate mixture to small bowl (mixture will be thick). Add remaining 2 tablespoons rum to mixture in saucepan; stir sauce to blend. Set aside.

✳ Position rack in center of oven. Preheat oven to 400°F. Line a baking sheet with parchment paper.

✳ Place 1 pastry sheet on floured work surface. Using 9-inch cake pan or plate as a guide, cut out a 9-inch circle. Repeat with remaining pastry sheet.

✳ Place 1 pastry round on prepared baking sheet; arrange 3 whole bananas on pastry, forming circle and leaving ½-inch pastry border. Fill in center with remaining bananas, cutting to fit. Pour any syrup from bananas and reserved 2 tablespoons chocolate mixture over bananas.

✳ Brush pastry edges with beaten egg. Top with second pastry round. Press edges to

 *Grand Desserts*

seal. Brush top with egg. Using small sharp knife, cut 8 vents in top of pastry to allow steam to escape. Freeze 10 minutes.

 Bake until pastry is golden and puffed, about 30 minutes. Run long knife under pastry to loosen. Cool on baking sheet on rack until just lukewarm, about 1½ hours. (Can be made 6 hours ahead. Let stand at room temperature.) Rewarm sauce over low heat. Serve pie with sauce. Makes 6–8 servings.

Lemon-Blackberry Cobblers with Lemon Sorbet

From the comfort of pastry to the bold flavors of blackberry and lemon—these sweet cobblers have so much going for them, it's hard to wait until dessert-time to tuck in.

½   of a 17.3-ounce package frozen puff pastry (1 sheet), thawed for 30 minutes
1   large egg yolk
1   tablespoon water
3   tablespoons fresh lemon juice
5½   teaspoons cornstarch
5   cups fresh or frozen, thawed (undrained) blackberries
1¼   cups sugar
1   pint lemon sorbet

✳ Preheat oven to 375°F.

✳ On a lightly floured surface roll out puff pastry sheet to a 14 x 13-inch rectangle. With 1 or more star-shaped cutters cut out 12 pastry stars.

✳ Place pastry stars on baking sheet lined with parchment paper. Freeze 5 minutes.

✳ Remove baking sheets from freezer. In a small bowl whisk egg yolk and water with a fork to blend. Brush top of each pastry star lightly with some egg wash (be careful not to drip down edges of pastry).

✳ Bake stars 10–14 minutes or until puffed and golden brown. Transfer pastry stars to a rack and cool completely. Keep oven on.

✳ In a large bowl whisk together lemon juice and cornstarch until combined well. Add blackberries and sugar, tossing gently to combine well. Divide berry mixture evenly among four 1½-cup shallow ramekins or baking dishes and put in 2 shallow baking pans.

✳ Bake berries 25 minutes. Cool slightly. Top each serving with pastry stars and serve, warm, with a scoop of lemon sorbet. Makes 4 servings.

Grand Desserts

Eccles Cake (Currant Pastries)

Eccles cakes are small, dome-shaped confections named for the township of Eccles in Lancashire, England. They typically have a buttery currant-dried fruit filling and are encased in puff pastry, as they are here.

¾	cup dried currants
⅓	cup dried cranberries
¼	cup packed golden brown sugar
2	tablespoons grated orange zest
3	tablespoons unsalted butter, room temperature
2	tablespoons fresh lemon juice
I	teaspoon grated lemon zest
½	teaspoon ground nutmeg
½	of a 17.3-ounce package frozen puff pastry (I sheet), thawed for 30 minutes
I	large egg, beaten to blend (for glaze)
2	teaspoons sugar

✳ In a medium bowl mix currants, cranberries, brown sugar, orange zest, butter, lemon juice, lemon zest, and nutmeg until well blended.

✳ Preheat oven to 375°F. Line a baking sheet with parchment paper.

✳ Roll out puff pastry on lightly floured surface into 12-inch square. Cut into four 6-inch squares. Place filling on half of each square, dividing equally. Brush edges of pastry with beaten egg. Fold pastry over filling, enclosing filling completely. Press edges firmly to seal. Transfer to prepared baking sheet. Brush with beaten egg and sprinkle with sugar.

✳ Bake pastries 18–21 minutes until deep golden brown. Transfer baking sheet to rack and cool pastries 5 minutes. Using metal spatula, carefully remove pastries from baking sheet. Cool. Makes 4 servings.

Apricot Galette

Happiness is a slice of apricot galette, warm from the oven and topped with lightly sweetened whipped cream.

¼	cup sliced almonds
¼	cup powdered sugar
6	fresh apricots (preferably slightly underripe)
½	of a 17.3-ounce package frozen puff pastry (1 sheet), thawed for 30 minutes
1½	tablespoons sugar
¼	teaspoon ground coriander
	Sweetened whipped cream (optional)

✳ Preheat oven to 425°F. Line a baking sheet with parchment paper.

✳ In a food processor pulse almonds with powdered sugar until finely ground. Pit apricots and cut into ⅛-inch-thick wedges.

✳ On a lightly floured surface unfold pastry sheet. Using a plate or cake pan as a guide, cut out a 9-inch round. Transfer round to prepared baking sheet. Prick pastry all over with a fork.

✳ Spoon almond mixture evenly over pastry, leaving a ¼-inch border. Decoratively arrange apricot wedges, overlapping them, on top of almond mixture. In a small cup combine sugar and coriander; sprinkle over almond mixture.

✳ Bake galette in middle of oven until edges are golden brown, about 30 minutes. Use the parchment paper to transfer galette to a rack to cool. Serve with sweetened whipped cream, if desired. Makes 6 servings.

Grand Desserts

Almond-Raspberry Jalousie

A jalousie is a small cake made with flaky pastry, filled with a layer of almond paste, and topped with jam. Here it is simplified with three readily available ingredients: refrigerated puff pastry, raspberry jam, and canned almond filling, which is easier to work with than almond paste. Look for the almond filling where pie fillings are shelved in the supermarket.

½   of a 17.3-ounce package frozen puff pastry (1 sheet), thawed for 30 minutes
¼   cup canned almond filling
¼   cup seedless raspberry jam or preserves, stirred to loosen
1   large egg
1   tablespoon milk

✳ Preheat oven to 375°F. Line a baking sheet with parchment paper.

✳ Roll out pastry on lightly floured surface to a 12x9-inch rectangle. Cut pastry in half lengthwise, creating two 12x4½-inch strips. Place 1 pastry strip on prepared baking sheet. Spread almond filling evenly over pastry, leaving ½-inch border on all sides. Dollop filling with jam; spread over filling (need not spread evenly).

✳ Fold remaining pastry strip in half lengthwise. Using small knife and beginning ½ inch from 1 end of pastry, cut slit through fold to within ½ inch of unfolded side of pastry.

✳ Repeat cutting slits at ½-inch intervals. Unfold dough and open flat on work surface. Whisk egg and milk in small bowl to blend. Brush cut pastry with some of egg mixture.

✳ Brush edges of jam-covered pastry strip with some of egg mixture. Place cut pastry strip over strip with jam, egg-glazed side up. Press edges firmly to seal.

✳ Bake tart until pastry is golden, about 22–25 minutes. Transfer sheet to rack and cool 5 minutes. Using parchment paper, slide tart onto rack and cool completely. Makes 6 servings.

Wrapped Pears with Vanilla Bean Sauce

Thanks to the convenience of frozen puff pastry, you can now duplicate this sublime restaurant experience at home. The pears are as stunning as they are delicious.

3	cups water
¾	cup sugar
½	vanilla bean, split
4	firm but ripe Bartlett or Bosc pears
½	cup heavy cream
½	of a 17.3-ounce package frozen puff pastry (1 sheet), thawed for 30 minutes
	Fresh raspberries

✳ In a medium, deep saucepan (large enough to hold 4 pears) heat water, sugar, and vanilla bean over low heat, stirring occasionally, until sugar is dissolved; bring to a boil.

✳ Using a melon baller, core pears from bottom and remove seeds. Peel pears, leaving stem intact. Cut a thin slice from bottom of each pear so it stands up. Place in pan. Reduce heat and simmer 10–20 minutes (it will depend on ripeness of pear), until tender, turning occasionally. Remove pears from syrup and refrigerate until cold, at least 1 hour.

✳ To make sauce, stir cream into syrup and boil 20–25 minutes until thickened and reduced to about ¾ cup; set aside. Remove vanilla bean, scraping seeds into sauce.

✳ Preheat oven to 400°F. Line a baking sheet with parchment paper.

✳ Unfold pastry sheet and cut into 8 strips, about ¾-inch wide. For each pear, join 2 strips by pressing ends together. Brush strips with cold water and sprinkle with sugar. Wind a strip of pastry around each pear, tucking end under bottom of pear. Place on prepared baking sheet. Cover tops of pears and pastry with aluminum foil to keep them from getting too browned. Bake 25–30 minutes, until pastry is puffed and browned.

✳ Heat vanilla bean sauce. Pool sauce on serving plates, place warm pears in center, and sprinkle with fresh raspberries. Makes 4 servings.

Grand Desserts

Mille-feuille is French for "a thousand leaves" and refers to a classic dessert made from whipped cream, custard, and jam or fruit puree sandwiched between multiple layers of crisp puff pastry and dusted with powdered sugar. Apricot is a heavenly choice of fruit filling, but any other fruit jam of choice will do.

2	cups whole milk
1	whole vanilla bean, split lengthwise
½	cup all-purpose flour
¾	cup sugar
1	pinch salt
6	large egg yolks
1	17.3-ounce packages frozen puff pastry (2 sheets), thawed for 30 minutes
½	cup apricot preserves
1–2	tablespoons powdered sugar

✳ In a small saucepan heat milk until small bubbles form. Drop in the vanilla bean, remove saucepan from heat, and set aside to cool until just warm. In a medium saucepan whisk the flour, sugar, salt, and egg yolks. Gradually whisk in warm milk. Simmer over medium-low heat until the custard thickens, stirring constantly with a wooden spoon to prevent sticking. Cool 10 minutes. Remove vanilla bean, scraping seeds into custard.

✳ Transfer custard to a bowl. Place a piece of plastic wrap on custard surface and allow to cool, stirring from time to time. (Can be made 1 day in advance.)

✳ Preheat oven to 400°F. Line 2 baking sheets with parchment paper.

✳ Roll out 1 of the puff pastry sheets on a lightly floured surface to 15x10-inch rectangle. Place the pastry onto a baking sheet, and prick all over with a fork. Repeat with second sheet of pastry.

✳ Bake in preheated oven for 24–27 minutes until puffed and golden. Remove from oven, and cool pastry on the baking sheet.

✳ Cut each cooled pastry sheet into 3 10x5-inch strips, making 6 strips total.

✳ Spread one strip thickly with custard. Place a second strip directly over the first; spread the top evenly with jam. Cover with the third strip, and dust with powdered sugar. Make a second stack with remaining 3 strips pastry, custard, and preserves. With a very sharp knife, cut each pastry into 4 rectangular portions. Makes 8 servings.

Grand Desserts ✳

Chocolate Hazelnut Marjolaine

A marjolaine is a long, rectangular French pastry, typically made with layers of dacquoise (a crisp, nut-flavored meringue) and layered with chocolate buttercream. This elegant dessert substitutes puff pastry for the dacquoise and a simplified chocolate-nut cream cheese filling for the buttercream, capturing the same look and flavors but with substantially less fuss.

½   of a 17.3-ounce package frozen puff pastry (1 sheet), thawed for 30 minutes

½   cup finely chopped hazelnuts

6   ounces semisweet chocolate, chopped

4   ounces cream cheese (half of an 8-ounce package), softened

½   cup packed light brown sugar

3   tablespoons strong brewed coffee, cold

1   cup ground hazelnuts

1   cup chilled heavy whipping cream

✳ Preheat oven to 450°F. Line a baking sheet with parchment paper.

✳ On a lightly floured surface roll out puff pastry to a 13-inch square. With a sharp knife, trim to 12 inches. Cut into 3 equal strips, 4 x 12 inches. Prick pastry all over with fork. Arrange on prepared baking sheet. Sprinkle with chopped hazelnuts, gently pressing nuts into pastry.

✳ Bake 8–10 minutes or until puffed and golden. Allow to cool. If not equal in size, trim with a serrated knife, using a gentle sawing motion.

✳ In a medium microwave bowl microwave chocolate for 1 minute. Stir until chocolate is melted. Cool to room temperature. In a large bowl beat together cream cheese, brown sugar, and coffee until smooth. Blend in melted chocolate. Fold in ground hazelnuts.

✳ In a large bowl whip cream until peaks form. Fold one-third of the whipped cream into the cheese mixture, then quickly fold in remaining whipped cream.

✳ Spread one-half of filling on a strip of puff pastry. Repeat layers, finishing with a puff pastry strip. Refrigerate for 3 hours or until set. With a serrated knife, cut into 8 slices using a gentle sawing motion. Makes 8 servings.

✳ Grand Desserts

Fruit Bundles with Brandy Custard Sauce

These luscious, autumnal fruit bundles are packed with the flavors of the season. The two-ingredient custard sauce is one of my kitchen secrets: melted ice cream, doctored with a hit of brandy. Be sure to choose a premium brand of ice cream for a rich, velvety sauce.

- ¾ cup pitted prunes, coarsely chopped
- ¾ cup dried apricots, coarsely chopped
- ¾ cup apple juice
- 1 medium-size Golden Delicious apple
- 1 tablespoon all-purpose flour
- ½ teaspoon ground cinnamon
- 5 tablespoons sugar, divided use
- 1 17.3-ounce package frozen puff pastry (2 sheets), thawed for 30 minutes
- ¾ pint (1½ cups) premium vanilla ice cream, melted
- 1 tablespoon brandy

❋ In a medium saucepan set over medium-high heat combine the prunes, apricots, and apple juice. Bring mixture to boiling. Reduce heat to low and simmer 8–10 minutes until fruit is soft and liquid is absorbed. Allow dried-fruit mixture to cool.

❋ Peel, core, and cut apple into ½-inch pieces. In large bowl combine apple, flour, cinnamon, cooled dried-fruit mixture, and 4 tablespoons sugar.

❋ Preheat oven to 425°F. Line a baking sheet with parchment paper.

❋ Unfold 1 sheet of pastry on lightly floured surface. Roll pastry out to a 12-inch square. Cut square into four 6-inch squares. Spoon one-eighth of fruit mixture onto center of each square.

❋ Brush edges of 1 pastry square with some water. Bring corners of pastry square over fruit mixture; gently squeeze and twist pastry together to seal in fruit filling and to form a bundle; fan out corners of pastry. Repeat to make 3 more bundles.

❋ Repeat with second sheet of pastry and remaining filling to make 4 more bundles. Place bundles, 2 inches apart, on prepared baking sheet.

❋ In a small bowl mix melted ice cream and brandy until blended. Cover and refrigerate.

❋ Brush tops of bundles with water, then sprinkle with remaining 1 tablespoon sugar. Bake 20–25 minutes until bundles are puffed and golden. Serve warm or remove bundles to wire rack to cool. Serve with custard sauce. Makes 8 servings.

Grand Desserts ❋

Pumpkin Pear Strudel

For a festive fall dessert, consider this strudel. It's a delicious cross between a pear pastry and pumpkin pie.

½   of a 17.3-ounce package frozen puff pastry (I sheet), thawed for 30 minutes
I   cup peeled, cored, and diced pears (about I medium pear)
½   cup solid pack pumpkin
⅓   cup packed light brown sugar
½   cup chopped pecans
¼   teaspoon ground ginger
⅛   teaspoon ground cloves
I   teaspoon ground cinnamon, divided use
I   large egg, lightly beaten
2   tablespoons sugar

❋ Preheat oven to 375°F. Line a baking sheet with parchment paper. Unfold pastry on a lightly floured surface.

❋ In a medium bowl combine pears, pumpkin, brown sugar, pecans, ginger, cloves, and ½ teaspoon of the cinnamon. Spoon one-half of filling in center third of one pastry sheet.

❋ Make downward slanting strips in outer sections of pastry (¾-inch apart) starting about I inch away from top of pastry and side of filling, cutting to outside edges. Starting at top, alternately fold left and right side pastry strips over filling forming a braid. Seal at top and bottom of strudel. Place on prepared baking sheet.

❋ Brush strudel with egg. In a small cup mix sugar with remaining ½ teaspoon cinnamon. Sprinkle pastry with cinnamon sugar.

❋ Bake 25–30 minutes or until golden brown and puffy. Serve warm. Makes 4–6 servings.

❋ *Grand Desserts*

Chocolate Macadamia Strudel

Is it any wonder chocolate is a favorite sweet? This dessert will halt any debate: warm melting chocolate and buttery-rich macadamias, all rolled up in flaky puff pastry.

1	large egg
1	tablespoon water
4	1-ounce squares bittersweet or semisweet baking chocolate, coarsely chopped
2	tablespoons milk
1	tablespoon butter
½	of a 17.3-ounce package frozen puff pastry (1 sheet), thawed for 30 minutes
1	cup chopped macadamia nuts
2	tablespoons powdered sugar

✳ Preheat oven to 375°F. Line a baking sheet with parchment paper. Mix egg and water in a small bowl.

✳ In a medium microwaveable bowl microwave chocolate, milk, and butter on high for 1½–2 minutes or until chocolate is almost melted, stirring after 1 minute. Stir until chocolate is completely melted. Cool slightly.

✳ Unfold pastry sheet onto lightly floured surface. Roll out to a 16 x 12-inch rectangle. Spread pastry evenly with chocolate mixture to within 1½ inches of edges. Sprinkle nuts over chocolate. Starting at short side, roll pastry sheet up jelly roll–style. Place, seam-side down, on prepared baking sheet. Tuck ends under to seal. Brush with egg mixture.

✳ Bake 32–35 minutes or until pastry is golden brown. Cool 30 minutes on baking sheet on wire rack. Sprinkle with powdered sugar. Makes 6 servings.

Piña Colada Pastry

This pastry satisfies my craving for fresh, tropical flavor—and with ingredients I keep on-hand in my pantry. As a plus, it's very easy to prepare.

1	large egg
1	tablespoon water
1	17.3-ounce package frozen puff pastry (2 sheets), thawed for 30 minutes
1	6-ounce package white baking chocolate squares, divided use
2	15-ounce cans pineapple chunks, well drained
⅔	cup sweetened flake coconut

✳ Preheat oven to 375°F. Line a baking sheet with parchment paper. Beat egg and water in small bowl.

✳ Unfold pastry sheets on lightly floured surface. Trim about 1 inch off each corner of each pastry sheet. Reserve trimmings to use as decorations. Place 1 pastry sheet on prepared baking sheet.

✳ Chop 4 of the white chocolate squares. In a medium bowl mix chopped chocolate, pineapple, and coconut. Spread pineapple mixture down center of prepared pastry sheet to within 1 inch of edges. Brush edges with water. Top with remaining pastry sheet. Press edges together with fork to seal. Decorate with reserved pastry trimmings, if desired. Brush with egg mixture. Cut several 2-inch slits, 2 inches apart, in top of pastry.

✳ Bake 32–35 minutes or until pastry is golden. Cool 30 minutes on baking sheet.

✳ In a small microwavable bowl melt remaining 2 chocolate squares on high for 1 minute. Drizzle over pastry. Let stand until chocolate is firm. Makes 10 servings.

✳ *Grand Desserts*

PIÑA COLADA PASTRY

Summer Fruit Cobbler

Midsummer marks high season at the local farmer's market. Make the most of the bounty of fruit with this quick-to-assemble, and utterly delicious, cobbler. Don't forget the vanilla ice cream!

8	cups of assorted ripe, sweet fruits such as peaches, plums, apricots, or blueberries
½	cup sugar
2	tablespoons cornstarch
¼	teaspoon cinnamon
⅛	teaspoon nutmeg
½	of a 17.3-ounce package frozen puff pastry (I sheet), thawed for 30 minutes
I	large egg
I	tablespoon water
3	tablespoons turbinado ("raw") sugar

✳ Preheat the oven to 350°F.

✳ In a large mixing bowl combine the fruit, sugar, cornstarch, cinnamon, and nutmeg. Pour the fruit mixture into a deep rectangular baking pan. Let the filling stand in the baking pan for at least 15 minutes before baking.

✳ In a small bowl beat together the egg and water to make an egg wash.

✳ Moisten the top edges of the pan. Place the puff pastry over the pan, sealing the edges of the pastry to the sides of the pan with fingertips. Brush the top of the pastry with the egg wash and sprinkle generously with turbinado sugar.

✳ Bake in the center of the preheated oven for 50 minutes to I hour or until the filling is bubbling and the puff pastry is puffy and golden brown. Makes 8–10 servings.

✔ **Cook's Note:** *The fruit filling should fill no more than two-thirds of the pan to avoid overflow when baked.*

Caramel Apple Dumplings

Inspired by a ubiquitous treat, this autumnal delight is a caramel-apple gone to finishing school.

⅔	cup pecan halves
1	cup jarred premium caramel ice cream topping, divided use
4	medium-small Golden Delicious apples (about 1¼ pounds total)
1	tablespoon fresh lemon juice
½	of a 17.3-ounce package frozen puff pastry (1 sheet), thawed for 30 minutes
1	large egg
1	tablespoon water
	Vanilla ice cream or lightly sweetened whipped cream (optional)

✳ Preheat oven to 375°F. Line a baking sheet with parchment paper.

✳ Set aside four pecan halves; chop remaining nuts. In a bowl mix chopped nuts with ¼ cup caramel sauce.

✳ Peel and core apples, creating a 1-inch-wide hollow from top to bottom. Place apples in a bowl and coat with lemon juice.

✳ On a lightly floured surface roll out puff pastry to a 14-inch square. Cut into 4 equal squares and center an apple upright on each. Push nut mixture equally into apple hollows.

✳ In a small cup whisk egg with water. Brush egg mixture over a ½-inch-wide border around each pastry; reserve remaining egg.

✳ To wrap each dumpling, with floured fingers bring two opposite pastry corners up over apple and pinch tips together. Repeat with remaining two corners. Firmly pinch all tips together; pinch each seam, then fold over about ⅛ inch along the seam and pinch again, leaving no holes. Space dumplings evenly on prepared baking sheet.

✳ Bake 20 minutes. Dip reserved pecan halves in egg mixture; press a nut half on top of each dumpling. Bake until pastry is deep golden, 10–15 minutes longer.

✳ With a wide spatula, transfer dumplings to plates. Accompany with remaining caramel sauce and ice cream or whipped cream, if desired. Makes 4 servings.

✔ **Cook's Note:** *The dumplings can be prepared ahead of time, up to the step of placing on the baking sheet. Cover and chill the sauce, dumplings, and egg mixture. Bake chilled dumplings as directed above.*

Grand Desserts

Coconut-Lime Cream Strudel

This luscious lime and coconut pastry is surprisingly easy to assemble and will transport your taste buds to the tropics.

½   of a 17.3-ounce package frozen puff pastry (1 sheet), thawed for 30 minutes

2   8-ounce packages cream cheese, softened

1   large egg

½   cup powdered sugar

1   tablespoon lime juice

2   teaspoons grated lime zest

⅔   cup sweetened flake coconut

1   tablespoon sugar

✳ Preheat oven to 400°F. Line a baking sheet with parchment paper.

✳ Unfold pastry on a lightly floured board and roll out to a 10x14-inch rectangle.

✳ In a medium bowl beat the cream cheese, egg, powdered sugar, lime juice, and lime zest with an electric mixer set on medium speed until well blended.

✳ Spoon cream cheese mixture down center of length of pastry to within 1 inch of each end; spread evenly to make a 4-inch-wide band. Sprinkle coconut evenly over cream cheese.

✳ Fold 1 long pastry edge over filling; brush top of edge with water. Fold remaining edge over filling, overlapping opposite side of pastry. Pinch pastry ends to seal.

✳ With 2 wide spatulas, gently lift the roll and lay, seam-side down, on prepared baking sheet. With a sharp knife, make shallow slashes at 1-inch intervals across the pastry. Sprinkle pastry evenly with sugar.

✳ Bake 24–28 minutes until strudel is deep golden brown. Let cool on pan at least 5 minutes. Serve warm or cool. Cut into 6 equal slices and transfer to plates. Makes 6 servings.

Apple Strudel

Warm, with a rich spiced apple filling and concentric layers of puff pastry, this apple strudel tastes every bit as grand as it looks.

1	large egg
1	tablespoon water
2	tablespoons brown sugar
1	tablespoon all-purpose flour
¼	teaspoon ground cinnamon
2	large Granny Smith apples, peeled, cored, and thinly sliced
2	tablespoons raisins, dried cranberries, or tart dried cherries
½	of a 17.3-ounce package frozen puff pastry (1 sheet), thawed for 30 minutes
2	tablespoons powdered sugar

✳ Preheat oven to 375°F. Line a baking sheet with parchment paper.

✳ In a small bowl mix the egg and water with a fork until blended.

✳ In a medium bowl mix the brown sugar, flour, and cinnamon. Add the apples and raisins; toss to coat.

✳ Unfold the pastry on a lightly floured surface and roll out to a 16x12-inch rectangle. With short side facing you, spoon apple mixture on bottom half of pastry to within 1 inch of edges.

✳ Starting at short side, roll up like a jelly roll. Place seam-side down on prepared baking sheet. Tuck ends under to seal. Brush with egg mixture. Cut several 2-inch long slits 2 inches apart on top.

✳ Bake 30–35 minutes or until golden. Cool on baking sheet on wire rack 30 minutes. Slice and serve warm. Sprinkle with powdered sugar. Makes 6 servings.

Bittersweet Chocolate Torte

I served this rich chocolate confection to an assembly of diehard chocoholics, to rave reviews. I was able to make it a couple of hours ahead and produce it out of the refrigerator when we gathered over coffee. The fresh raspberries push it over the top.

½ of a 17.3-ounce package frozen puff pastry (I sheet), thawed for 30 minutes
I large egg yolk
I pound bittersweet or semisweet chocolate, coarsely chopped
I cup heavy whipping cream
I teaspoon vanilla extract
I pint raspberries
Lightly sweetened whipped cream

* Preheat oven to 425°F.

* Unfold pastry on lightly floured surface and roll out to a 12-inch square. Cut off corners to make a rough circle. Press pastry into 9-inch springform pan. Prick pastry all over with fork.

* Bake for 18–21 minutes or until golden. Cool in pan on wire rack.

* Place egg yolk into small bowl; set aside.

* Place chocolate and cream in a medium saucepan over medium-low heat. Cook and stir until chocolate melts, stirring until smooth. Remove from heat and whisk in the vanilla. Pour some chocolate mixture into bowl with egg yolk and stir well. Return egg mixture to remaining chocolate mixture and stir well. Cook and stir I minute. Cool. Pour mixture into pastry crust. Cover and refrigerate until firm, about 2 hours.

* Cut into slices and garnish with raspberries and sweetened whipped cream. Makes 6–8 servings.

Grand Desserts *

Marlborough Pie (Apple Custard Tart)

Marlborough pie—a custard confection made with applesauce and sherry—is a Massachusetts specialty. It's traditionally served at Thanksgiving, but you can make it any time you're craving sweet comfort.

¾	cup good-quality applesauce
¾	cup sugar
¾	cup sweet sherry
6	tablespoons melted butter
4	large eggs, lightly beaten
½	cup heavy cream
I	tablespoon fresh lemon juice
I	teaspoon ground nutmeg
½	of a I7.3-ounce package frozen puff pastry (I sheet), thawed for 30 minutes

✳ Preheat oven to 350°F.

✳ In a medium bowl whisk the applesauce, sugar, sherry, melted butter, eggs, heavy cream, lemon juice, and nutmeg until well blended.

✳ Unfold the puff pastry sheet. Press pastry into an 8-inch pie plate, tucking ends over to form crust.

✳ Pour apple mixture into the pie crust, smoothing top.

✳ Bake about 45–50 minutes or until filling is set. (It will look similar to a pumpkin pie.) Transfer to wire rack and cool slightly. Serve warm or room temperature. Makes 6–8 servings.

Grand Desserts

Who doesn't like chocolate? These puffed bundles make a trip to chocolate heaven a breeze. For a delicious twist, try white or milk chocolate chips, both in the bundles and in the ganache, in place of the semisweet chips.

⅓   cup chopped pecans (or walnuts)

2   cups semisweet chocolate chips, divided use

½   of a 17.3-ounce package frozen puff pastry (I sheet), thawed for 30 minutes

2   tablespoons powdered sugar

½   cup heavy cream

I   pint fresh raspberries

     Sweetened whipped cream (optional)

     Mint sprigs (optional)

✳ Preheat oven to 400°F. Line a baking sheet with parchment paper.

✳ Mix the nuts and I⅓ cups chocolate chips in a small bowl.

✳ Unfold pastry on lightly floured surface and roll out to a 12-inch square. Cut into four 6-inch squares.

✳ Place one-fourth of the chocolate mixture in center of each square. Brush edges of squares with water. Fold corners to center on top of filling and twist tightly to seal. Fan out corners. Place 2 inches apart on baking sheet.

✳ Bake 13–15 minutes or until golden.

✳ While bundles bake, make the chocolate ganache by placing the heavy cream in a small saucepan set over medium heat. Bring to a simmer. Place the remaining ⅔ cup semisweet chocolate chips in a small bowl and pour hot cream over top. Whisk until smooth.

✳ Remove bundles from baking sheet. Cool on wire rack 10 minutes. Pour some ganache onto a plate and place I bundle on top. Sprinkle with raspberries. Garnish with whipped cream and mint sprigs, if desired. Makes 4 servings.

Grand Desserts ✳

Pain Abricot (Apricot Streusel Tart)

This simplified variation on a classic French tart is a masterful mix of textures: the crust bakes up crisp and light, giving way to the velvet-y texture of the apricot topping, studded with bits of crunchy gingersnaps.

1	large egg
1	tablespoon water
9	packaged gingersnap cookies, crushed
2	tablespoons sugar
1	teaspoon ground cinnamon
2	tablespoons butter, melted
½	of a 17.3-ounce package frozen puff pastry (1 sheet), thawed for 30 minutes
2	15-ounce cans apricot halves, drained and patted dry between paper towels

✳ Preheat oven to 375°F. Line a pizza pan or baking sheet with parchment paper.

✳ Mix egg and water in a small bowl. In another small bowl mix cookie crumbs, sugar, cinnamon, and butter.

✳ Unfold pastry on lightly floured surface and roll out to a 13-inch square. Trim to 13-inch circle. Place on prepared pan or baking sheet. Fold over ¾ of outer edge to make rim. Brush with egg mixture. Top with apricot halves, cut-side down, overlapping slightly if necessary. Sprinkle with cookie mixture.

✳ Bake 32–35 minutes or until pastry is golden. Cool in pan on wire rack. Cut into wedges. Makes 6 servings.

Grand Desserts

PAIN ABRICOT

Strawberry Lemon Cream Tart

Sweet strawberries in their prime and a tart lemon cream—you just can't go wrong with the combination of these two stellar elements.

I	large egg
I	tablespoon water
½	of a 17.3-ounce package frozen puff pastry (I sheet), thawed for 30 minutes
I	tablespoon coarse or regular sugar
½	cup chilled heavy whipping cream
⅓	cup jarred lemon curd
I	pint basket strawberries, hulled and halved through stem end
¼	cup red currant jelly

✳ Preheat oven to 350°F. Line a baking sheet with parchment paper. In a small bowl mix the egg and water.

✳ On lightly floured surface roll out pastry sheet to a 14x11-inch rectangle. Cut four (4) 1-inch-wide strips off short side and four 1-inch strips off long side. Transfer pastry rectangle to prepared baking sheet. Pierce with fork. Brush with some of egg mixture.

✳ Arrange I pastry strip on each edge of rectangle so outside edges meet, trimming as necessary, forming tart edges. Brush top of strips with egg glaze. Repeat with remaining pastry strips. Brush top of strips with egg and sprinkle with sugar.

✳ Bake tart 5 minutes. Pierce pastry inside border edges with fork if puffed. Continue baking until golden brown, about 18–20 minutes. Cool completely.

✳ Just before serving, whip the cream to stiff peaks in a medium bowl with an electric mixer set on high speed. Place lemon curd in another medium bowl. Stir in half of the whipped cream. Fold in remaining cream. Spread cream mixture in tart. Arrange strawberries atop lemon cream in rows, cut-side down.

✳ Melt the jelly in a small saucepan set over low heat; brush over berries. Cut into pieces. Makes 6 servings.

Grand Desserts ✳

Peach Melba Bundles with Orange Custard Sauce

It's hard to think of a better use for puff pastry than scooping up this luxurious, orange-scented custard sauce. But the main event is the peach-raspberry filling in the bundles, a combination originally dreamt up by the famous French chef Escoffier for the popular opera singer Dame Nellie Melba.

½ cup heavy whipping cream

½ cup whole milk

1 teaspoon grated orange zest

3 large egg yolks

9 tablespoons sugar, divided use

1 17.3-ounce package frozen puff pastry (2 sheets), thawed for 30 minutes

1 pound fresh peaches, peeled, pitted, and chopped (frozen peaches may be substituted)

½ cup fresh raspberries

2 tablespoons all purpose flour

½ teaspoon fresh lemon juice

1 large egg white, whisked until frothy

✳ Combine cream, milk, and orange zest in small heavy saucepan. Bring to simmer. Remove from heat. Cover and let steep 15 minutes.

✳ In a medium bowl whisk yolks and 4 tablespoons sugar to blend. Gradually whisk warm milk mixture into yolk mixture; return to saucepan. Cook over medium-low heat until mixture coats back of spoon and leaves path when finger is drawn across, stirring constantly, about 7 minutes (do not boil). Pour into bowl. Place plastic wrap directly on surface and chill until cold, whisking occasionally, about 3 hours.

✳ Line baking sheet with parchment paper. On a lightly floured surface roll out 1 pastry sheet to a 13-inch square. Using 6-inch-diameter bowl as guide, cut out 4 circles. Transfer circles to prepared sheet; cover with plastic. Repeat with second pastry sheet. Transfer pastry circles to same baking sheet, placing atop plastic wrap. Freeze 10 minutes.

✳ In a medium bowl toss the peaches, raspberries, flour, lemon juice, and 3 tablespoons of remaining sugar. Roll out pastry circles on lightly floured surface to 7-inch-diameter rounds. Place ¼ cup fruit mixture in center of each round. Gather dough atop fruit and twist and pinch firmly to enclose completely. Place on baking sheet. Freeze bundles at least 15 minutes.

* Preheat oven to 400°F. Brush bundles all over with egg white and sprinkle each with some of the remaining 2 tablespoons sugar. Bake until golden, about 20–22 minutes. Cool on baking sheet on rack at least 10 minutes.

* Place 2 tablespoons sauce in center of each of 8 plates. Place 1 bundle in center of each plate and serve warm. Makes 8 servings.

Heirloom Pear Hand Pies with Brown Sugar & Brandy

Old-fashioned and irresistible, these humble hand pies make the most of autumn's fruit bounty.

    Butter
2½   pounds ripe but firm Bartlett pears, peeled, cored and cut into ½-inch dice
½   cup packed dark brown sugar
2   tablespoons fresh lemon juice
2   tablespoons brandy
1   teaspoon vanilla extract
1   17.3-ounce package frozen puff pastry (2 sheets), thawed for 30 minutes
2   egg whites, lightly beaten with 1 teaspoon cold water
2   tablespoons sugar
1   pint vanilla ice cream, for serving (optional)

✻ In a large skillet melt the butter over high heat. Add the diced pears and cook, stirring occasionally, until they are golden around the edges, about 5 minutes. Add the brown sugar, lemon juice, and the brandy. Cook until the pears are tender and the liquid in the skillet has reduced to about 2 tablespoons, 4–5 minutes. Stir in vanilla. Spread the diced pears on a baking sheet and let cool, about 25 minutes.

✻ On a lightly floured surface roll out 1 of the puff pastry sheets to a 9 x 14-inch rectangle. Using a plate as a template, carefully cut out two 7-inch rounds. Transfer the rounds to a large baking sheet lined with parchment paper. Repeat with second puff pastry sheet.

✻ Spoon one-fourth of the pear filling over half of a pastry round, leaving a ½-inch border at the edge. Brush the border lightly with the egg-white wash. Fold the top half of the round over and press the edges together firmly to seal. Repeat with the remaining pear filling and pastry rounds. Refrigerate the hand pies for 30 minutes. Reserve the remaining egg-white wash.

✻ Preheat the oven to 425°F. Brush the tops of the hand pies lightly with the remaining egg-white wash. Sprinkle the tops all over with the sugar.

✻ Bake the hand pies for 15 minutes in the middle of the oven, then reduce the oven temperature to 400° and bake the hand pies for about 14–17 minutes longer, until they are a deep golden brown color. Let the hand pies cool for 20 minutes. Serve warm with vanilla ice cream, if desired. Makes 4 servings.

✔ **Cook's Note:**

The hand pies can be made one day ahead and kept at room temperature. To serve, reheat the pies in a 350° oven for 10 minutes.

Black Forest Jalousie

The rich combination of chocolate and cherries in this French confection makes an unforgettable finish to an elegant meal. For a gussy flourish, use a vegetable peeler to shave more chocolate, from a bar or block, over the top of the dessert.

1	17.3-ounce package frozen puff pastry (2 sheets), thawed for 30 minutes
1	21-ounce can cherry pie filling
¼	cup sliced almonds
½	cup miniature semisweet chocolate chips
1	large egg, lightly beaten
2	teaspoons sugar
	Lightly sweetened whipped cream (optional)

✳ Preheat oven to 375°. Line a baking sheet with parchment paper.

✳ Unfold 1 pastry sheet. Cut sheet in half across width. On lightly floured surface roll one half into 15x7-inch rectangle. Roll the other half into 14x6-inch rectangle. Fold larger rectangle lengthwise in half. Along fold, cut parallel slits, ½ inch apart, 2½ inches long; unfold.

✳ Place the smaller rectangle on prepared baking sheet. Top with half of the cherry pie filling, leaving a 1-inch border all around. Sprinkle with half the almonds and half the chips. Brush edges of pastry around filling with some of the egg. Top with the remaining, larger slit pastry; align and press edges to seal. Brush top with egg. Sprinkle with half the sugar.

✳ Repeat with remaining pastry sheet, pie filling, almonds, chips, egg, and sugar.

✳ Bake in 375° oven for 32–35 minutes or until puffed and golden brown. Transfer to wire rack and let cool 15–20 minutes to serve warm. Or let cool to room temperature. Serve with whipped cream, if desired. Makes 8 servings.

✔ **Cook's Note:** *The pastries can be assembled, tightly wrapped, and frozen for up to 1 month. Before baking, let thaw in refrigerator overnight.*

Grand Desserts

Index

Index

Notes

_____   _____

_____   _____

_____   _____

_____   _____

_____   _____

_____   _____

_____   _____

_____   _____

_____   _____

_____   _____

_____   _____